DESIGN for OBAMA

by **AARON PERRY-ZUCKER** & **SPIKE LEE** with **STEVEN HELLER**

DESIGN
for
OBAMA

TASCHEN

BLACKBURN COLLEGE
LIBRARY
Acc No. BB28378
Class No. UCL 741.674 ZUK
Date OCT 09

TABLE of CONTENTS

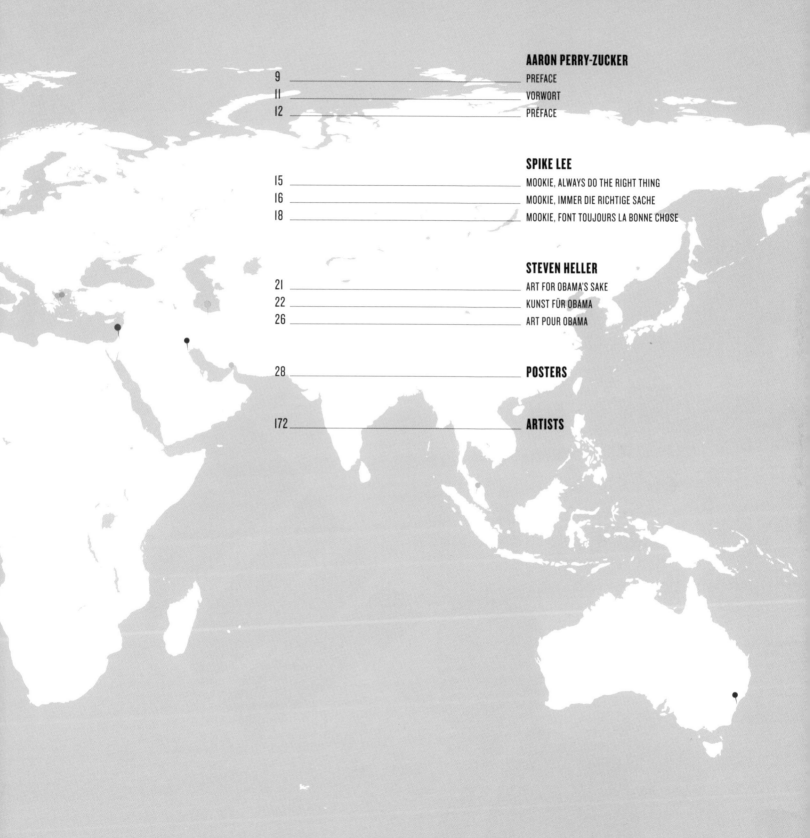

ESSAYS

THE ONES
BEEN WAITING FOR.
HOPE
AMBITION
IMAGINE
ONE
WE CAN BUILD
MORALS STAND
STRENGTH
YOU
CAUSE
NATION FORWARD

This whole thing started the summer leading up to the 2008 election, one week before the beginning of my senior year at Rhode Island School of Desgin (RISD). I was most likely sitting on the floor in the TV nook of my friend's apartment that I was subletting, drinking my fourth root beer of the day, watching *Law & Order* reruns, and reading *Design Observer*, a popular design community blog. *Design Observer* posed two simple questions to its readers: Would you like to own designersforobama.org? What would you do with it?

I had been working on the campaign for over a year as the graphic designer for Students for Obama, the student outreach program of Obama for America. The work, while necessary, wasn't very stimulating or complex, and consisted of designing collateral for student groups in every state. I had been determined to do something more for the campaign, something that used design in a better way, but I didn't have any idea how to do this until *Design Observer* actually posed the question.

The Obama campaign found incredible success in using the Internet as a means of organically growing a grassroots army, the energy of which swept Obama into the White House. If we wanted to do the same for the design community (in the broadest sense possible) then it seemed logical to use the same tools. I was sure that a venue for displaying posters and providing free and easy means for regular people to print out large-scale, tiled posters could galvanize creative communities and spread a lot of high-quality campaign posters made by and for the campaign.

With the help of my good friend and accomplice, Adam Meyer, who also just graduated from RISD, Design for Obama was designed, built, and launched within a week. We sent a brief press release to a number of design, social media, and political blogs that linked back to our gallery. The word spread fast, and soon it was all I could do to keep up with the dozens of posters that would come in every day, each of which had to be sized and sorted correctly. I was astounded: The level of

quality of the posters ranged but overall was surprisingly high, and the people who were submitting were more diverse than I could have dreamed; every person had a story and a point of view, and this came through in their work.

We continued to build steam and reached the high point of appearing in a *New York Times* syndicated article by the famous design author Steven Heller. The next thing I knew,

I was sitting in class when I got a call from Spike Lee. We spoke for 20 minutes and he told me that Design for Obama was an excellent project and that the second he saw it he knew it had to be published. With his help and the efforts of the good people at TASCHEN, we have done just that. Please enjoy this book of posters / historical document capturing the energy, excitement, and hope we experienced as we all worked to elect Barack Obama.

VORWORT von AARON PERRY-ZUCKER

Die ganze Sache fing im Sommer vor den amerikanischen Präsidentschaftswahlen 2008 an, kurz bevor mein letztes Studienjahr an der Rhode Island School of Design (RISD) losging. Die meiste Zeit hielt ich mich in der Fernsehecke der Wohnung meines Freundes auf, in der ich zur Untermiete wohnte, saß auf dem Boden, trank Malzbier, schaute mir alte Folgen von „Law & Order" an und las den *Design Observer*, einen unter Designern beliebten Blog. Der *Design Observer* stellte seinen Lesern zwei einfache Fragen: Wollt ihr die Domain „designersforobama.org" haben? Und wenn ja, was würdet ihr damit anstellen?

Der Obama-Wahlkampf hatte ungemein großen Erfolg damit, via Internet eine riesengroße basisdemokratische Bewegung aufzubauen, von deren Energie Obama letztendlich auch ins Weiße Haus getragen wurde. Wenn wir das Gleiche für die Designinteressierten im weitesten Sinne tun wollten, schien es nur logisch, dieselben Mittel einzusetzen. Ich war mir sicher, dass es viele Menschen zur Kreativität anspornen würde, wenn eine kostenlose und einfache Möglichkeit zur Bereitstellung von großen, aus mehreren Stücken zusammengesetzten Plakaten geschaffen würde, die sich jeder selbst ausdrucken konnte. Auf diese

tern, die jeden Tag auf der Website eintrafen, zu sortieren und auf die richtige Größe zu skalieren. Ich war verblüfft, nicht nur über die Qualität der eingereichten Plakate (die variierte, aber generell erstaunlich hoch war), sondern besonders darüber, wie unterschiedlich der Background der Einsender war. Jeder hatte seine Story und seinen ganz eigenen Standpunkt, den er mit der Arbeit zum Ausdruck bringen wollte.

Die Sache gewann immer mehr an Fahrt und erlebte einen Höhepunkt, als sie in der *New York Times* von dem berühmten Designkritiker Steven Heller besprochen wurde.

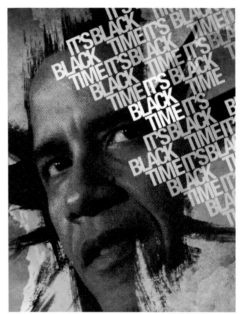

Ich engagierte mich zu diesem Zeitpunkt schon seit über einem Jahr im Wahlkampf und unterstützte als Grafikdesigner die *Students for Obama*, den studentischen Ableger der Kampagne *Obama for America*. Die Arbeit bestand hauptsächlich darin, Werbematerial für studentische Gruppen in jedem Bundesstaat zu entwerfen und war zwar notwendig, aber nicht besonders interessant oder anspruchsvoll. Ich war fest entschlossen, mehr für die Kampagne zu tun, etwas, wobei Design auf eine bessere Art und Weise eingesetzt werden konnte, aber mir war bisher nichts eingefallen – bis der *Design Observer* mir diese ganz konkrete Frage stellte.

Weise würde eine Menge guter Wahlkampfplakate in Umlauf kommen, die von und für die Kampagne entstanden sind.

Mithilfe meines guten Freundes und Komplizen Adam Meyer, der mittlerweile ebenfalls sein Studium an der RISD abgeschlossen hat, wurde die Website *Design for Obama* innerhalb einer Woche gestaltet und ins Netz gestellt. Beim Launch schickten wir eine kurze Pressemeldung an eine Reihe von sozialen Netzwerken, Design- und Politikblogs, die einen Link auf unsere Galerie schalteten. Die Neuigkeit sprach sich schnell herum, und schon bald hatte ich alle Hände voll damit zu tun, die Dutzenden von Pos-

Eines Tages saß ich in der Uni im Seminar, als mein Handy klingelte. Ich wollte meinen Ohren nicht trauen: Spike Lee war dran und erzählte mir zwanzig Minuten lang, was für ein hervorragendes Projekt *Design for Obama* sei und dass er, schon als er es zum ersten Mal sah, gedacht habe, dass es veröffentlicht werden muss. Mit seiner Hilfe und dank der Bemühungen des wunderbaren Teams von TASCHEN haben wir genau das getan. Wir wünschen viel Freude an diesem Buch. Diese Plakate sind historische Dokumente, die von der Energie, Begeisterung und Hoffnung zeugen, mit der wir uns alle zusammen für Barack Obamas Präsidentschaft eingesetzt haben.

PRÉFACE par AARON PERRY-ZUCKER

Toute cette histoire a commencé l'été précédant les élections de 2008, une semaine avant le début de ma dernière année à l'École de design de Rhode Island. J'étais assis par terre dans le coin télé de l'appartement que je sous-louais à un ami, sans doute en train de boire ma quatrième bière de la journée devant des rediffusions de *New York Police judiciaire*, tout en lisant *Design Observer*, un blog communautaire de qualité consacré au design. *Design Observer* posait deux questions simples à ses lecteurs : Aimeriez-vous posséder le site designersforobama.org ? Qu'en feriez-vous ?

faire croître de façon quasi organique une armée de la base, dont l'énergie a propulsé Obama jusqu'à la Maison-Blanche. Si nous voulions faire la même chose pour la communauté du design (dans le sens le plus large possible), il semblait logique d'utiliser les mêmes outils. J'étais certain qu'un support présentant des créations graphiques que les internautes pourraient télécharger et imprimer facilement et gratuitement galvaniserait la communauté artistique et permettrait de diffuser un grand nombre d'images de qualité conçues par et pour la campagne.

pu le rêver. Chacune de ces personnes avait une histoire et un point de vue, ce qui se ressentait dans leur travail.

Nous avons continué sur notre lancée jusqu'à obtenir la reconnaissance suprême d'être cité par le célèbre spécialiste du design Steven Heller dans un article du *New York Times*. Sans que je comprenne ce qui m'arrivait, alors que j'étais en cours, j'ai reçu un coup de téléphone de Spike Lee. Nous avons parlé pendant environ 20 minutes et il m'a dit que Design for Obama était un excellent projet et que, dès qu'il en avait entendu parler, il avait compris que cet ensemble d'œuvres devait être publié.

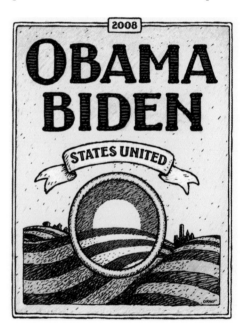

J'étais engagé dans la campagne depuis plus d'un an en tant que graphiste pour Students for Obama, la branche d'Obama for America destinée à sensibiliser les étudiants. Ce travail, bien que nécessaire, n'était ni très stimulant ni très compliqué, et consistait à créer des plaquettes pour les groupes universitaires présents dans les différents États. J'étais déterminé à m'impliquer davantage dans la campagne, en utilisant le design d'une meilleure manière, mais je n'avais aucune idée de comment m'y prendre, jusqu'à ce que *Design Observer* pose la question concrètement.

La campagne d'Obama rencontrait un succès incroyable en utilisant Internet pour

Avec mon ami et complice Adam Meyer, qui venait de sortir de la RISD, nous avons conçu, créé et lancé Design for Obama en une semaine. Nous avons envoyé un bref communiqué de presse à un certain nombre de titres de la presse généraliste et spécialisée dans le design, ainsi qu'à des blogs politiques qui ont renvoyé leurs lecteurs sur notre galerie. La nouvelle s'est vite répandue : j'ai bientôt été débordé par les dizaines d'affiches qui arrivaient chaque jour et qu'il fallait mettre en page et trier correctement. J'étais stupéfait : la qualité de ces graphismes était variable, mais globalement plutôt élevée, et ils provenaient de gens plus différents que je n'aurais

Grâce à son aide et aux efforts de la merveilleuse équipe de TASCHEN, c'est ce que nous avons fait. J'espère que vous prendrez plaisir à feuilleter ce livre d'affiches / document historique qui saisit l'énergie, l'excitation et l'espoir que nous avons ressentis en œuvrant tous pour l'élection de Barack Obama.

MOOKIE, ALWAYS DO THE RIGHT THING by SPIKE LEE

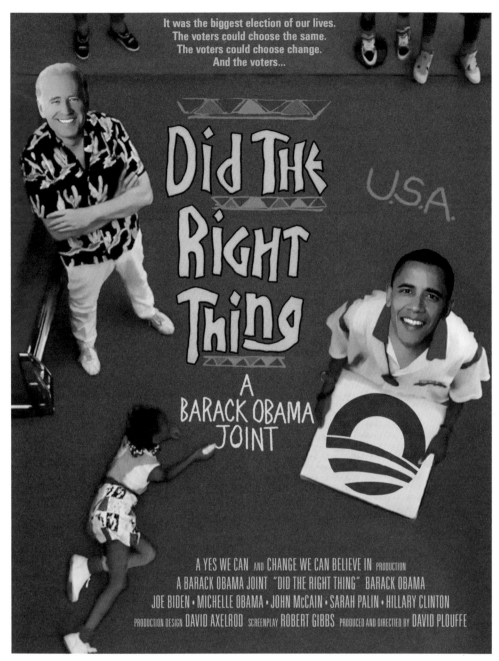

what he had was a book, about my relationship with TASCHEN, and that we should partner to get this done.

Even before I knew I wanted to be a film-maker, I had always been interested in graph-ics—not just movie posters, I also loved album covers and T-shirts. Often when there were no cops around, I would take down my favorite movie posters off of the subway trains and put them up in my room. When I became a film-maker, I wanted to have a good deal of creative input in my film posters. I wanted the artwork to effectively convey the spirit and soul of the film it was trying to sell. But I wanted it to be done in a creative way. I wanted people to be like I was—someone who was so moved by that poster that they would tear it off of a wall or a subway train and hang it up in their room. That's how hyped I wanted my posters to be. I just could not understand why people made the same, old, tired, and boring poster again and again. Shoot me please.

Art Sims, as for most of my films, created the poster for *Do the Right Thing*. He heads 11:24 Design Advertising, the lone African American company working in Hollywood today. Art has done and continues to do great work. *Did the Right Thing* was created by Don Button, a professor of graphic communica-tions at Sacramento City College. Mr. Button's poster is one of many included in this unique collection of political art; it's a collection that contributed to Barack Hussein Obama becom-ing the 44th President of the United States and the first African American to hold the office; a collection that shows what artists everywhere have always done and will continue to do —change the way we see things.

Leah Hamilton, the art buyer at my advertising agency, SpikeDDB, called me over to her desk, "Spike, check this out." She was looking at her computer screen as I walked over. "What's up?" I asked. "Somebody is biting your *Do the Right Thing* poster," she answered. I looked at her screen and was amazed. Somebody had stuck Joe Biden's head on Danny Aiello's head, Barack Obama's head on mine, and retitled it, *Did the Right Thing*. I was laughing like a

mad man. I asked Leah to track down who did this and where it came from. After some quick investigative work on Leah's part, she came up with a whole website of outstanding Obama posters, and a name—Aaron Perry-Zucker. I quickly sent an email to Aaron, who got right back to me with his phone number. Aaron told me he was a senior at RISD, and the whole story behind the website. We agreed to meet in New York, and that's where I told him that

MOOKIE, IMMER DIE RICHTIGE SACHE von SPIKE LEE

Leah Hamilton, die in meiner Werbeagentur SpikeDDB für Illustrationen zuständig ist, rief mich herüber zu ihrem Schreibtisch: „Guck dir das mal an, Spike." Sie sah auf ihren Bildschirm, als ich zu ihr kam. „Was gibt's?", fragte ich. „Da hat jemand dein Plakat von *Do the Right Thing* verwurstet", antwortete sie. Ich sah auf ihren Bildschirm und war erst mal sprachlos. Jemand hatte den Kopf von Barack Obama auf meinen Körper montiert, den Kopf von Joe Biden auf den von Danny Aiello und dem Ganzen dann die neue Überschrift gegeben: *Did the Right Thing* („Das haben wir richtig gemacht!").

TASCHEN und dass wir uns zusammen dieses Projekt vorknöpfen sollten.

Ich habe mich immer schon für Grafikdesign interessiert, noch bevor ich wusste, dass ich Filmemacher werden wollte – nicht nur für Filmplakate, sondern auch für Schallplattencover und T-Shirts. Wenn gerade kein Polizist in der Nähe war, habe ich oft die Plakate meiner Lieblingsfilme in U-Bahnwaggons abgerissen und mir zu Hause ins Zimmer gehängt. Als ich Filmemacher wurde, war es mir sehr wichtig, so viel kreativen Einfluss wie möglich auf meine Filmplakate auszuüben. Ich wollte, dass die Plakatgestaltung die Stimmung und

Werbeagentur 11:24 Design Advertising, der einzigen afroamerikanischen Agentur, die es heutzutage in Hollywood gibt. Art entwirft hervorragende Sachen. *Did the Right Thing* ist das Werk von Don Button, einem Professor für visuelle Kommunikation am Sacramento City College. Buttons Poster ist eines von vielen, das in dieser einmaligen Sammlung politischer Kunst zu finden ist: Es ist eine Sammlung, die dazu beigetragen hat, dass Barack Hussein Obama der 44. Präsident der Vereinigten Staaten von Amerika geworden ist, der erste Afroamerikaner, der dieses Amt innehat. Eine Samm-

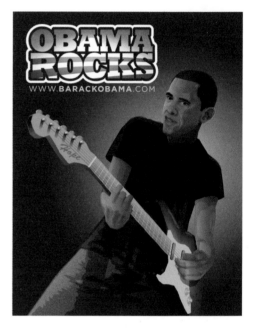

Ich lachte mich halb tot. Ich bat Leah herauszufinden, wer sich das ausgedacht hatte und woher das Poster stammte. Nach einer kurzen Internetrecherche stieß Leah auf eine ganze Website mit bemerkenswerten Obama-Plakaten – und auf einen Namen: Aaron Perry-Zucker. Ich schickte Aaron sofort eine E-Mail, worauf er mir seine Telefonnummer zurückmailte. Ich erfuhr, dass er Student an der Rhode Island School of Design war und was hinter der Idee mit der Website steckte. Wir verabredeten uns in New York und ich schlug ihm dann vor, ein Buch aus dem Ganzen zu machen. Ich erzählte ihm von meiner Zusammenarbeit mit

den Geist des Films wirklich vermittelte – und zwar auf kreative Art und Weise. Ich wollte, dass die Leute sich genauso verhielten wie ich – dass sie sich so stark von dem Plakat angesprochen fühlten, dass sie es von der Wand reißen oder aus der U-Bahn mitnehmen und sich ins Zimmer hängen würden. Meine Poster sollten abgefahrene Kultobjekte sein. Ich konnte einfach nicht nachvollziehen, warum dieselben müden, zum Gähnen langweiligen Plakate immer und immer wieder gemacht wurden.

Art Sims gestaltete das Plakat für *Do the Right Thing*, ebenso wie für die meisten anderen meiner Filme. Er ist der Chef der

lung, die zeigt, was Künstler zu allen Zeiten getan haben und immer tun werden: Sie verändern unsere Sicht auf die Welt.

MOOKIE, FONT TOUJOURS LA BONNE CHOSE par SPIKE LEE

Un jour, Leah Hamilton, la responsable des acquisitions artistiques de mon agence de publicité SpikeDDB, me demande de venir voir quelque chose à son bureau : «Spike, regarde un peu ça!» Elle travaillait à son ordinateur, alors je m'approche et je lui demande : «Qu'est-ce qui se passe?» Et là, elle me dit : «Quelqu'un a détourné ton affiche pour *Do the Right Thing*.» J'ai regardé son écran et j'ai cru halluciner. Quelqu'un avait collé le visage de Barack Obama sur la tête de Danny Aiello et

celui de Joe Biden sur la mienne, et changé le titre en *Did the Right Thing*. Je me suis mis à rire comme un fou. J'ai demandé à Leah de retrouver la personne qui avait fait ça et de découvrir d'où ça venait. Après une petite enquête, Leah a déniché tout un site Internet présentant d'excellentes affiches pour Obama, et un nom – Aaron Perry-Zucker. J'ai tout de suite envoyé un mail à Aaron, qui m'a renvoyé son numéro de téléphone. Aaron m'a expliqué qu'il était en dernière année à la RISD et m'a

raconté l'histoire de son site. Nous avons pris rendez-vous et nous nous sommes rencontrés à New York. C'est là que je lui ai dit qu'il avait un livre entre les mains, que j'avais de bonnes relations avec TASCHEN et que nous devrions nous associer pour mener à bien ce projet.

Même avant de savoir que je voulais faire des films, j'ai toujours été très intéressé par le graphisme – pas seulement celui des affiches de film, j'adorais aussi les pochettes de disque ou les tee-shirts. Souvent, quand il n'y avait pas de flics dans le coin, j'allais dans le métro pour arracher les affiches de mes films préférés et les mettre dans ma chambre. Quand je suis devenu réalisateur, j'ai tenu à ce que mes affiches de film soient des créations travaillées et originales. Je voulais que leur conception artistique porte l'esprit et l'âme du film que j'essayais de vendre, mais je voulais que ce soit fait de façon novatrice. Je voulais que les gens aient la même réaction que moi – qu'ils soient si touchés par cette affiche qu'ils aient envie de l'arracher du mur ou du métro pour l'accrocher dans leur chambre. Je n'arrivais pas à comprendre pourquoi les gens continuaient à produire les mêmes affiches vieillottes, éculées et barbantes. Non mais franchement!

C'est Art Sims qui a créé l'affiche de *Do the Right Thing*, et la plupart de celles de mes autres films. Il dirige l'agence 11:24 Design Advertising, la seule entreprise afro-américaine à travailler pour Hollywood aujourd'hui. Art a toujours fait du bon boulot, et continue. *Did the Right Thing* est une création de Don Button, professeur de communication graphique au Sacramento City College. L'affiche de M. Button fait partie de la vaste et unique collection d'art politique que présente ce livre. Ces œuvres ont contribué à ce que Barack Hussein Obama deviennent le 44e président des États-Unis et le premier Afro-américain à occuper ce poste suprême. Elles démontrent ce que les artistes du monde entier font depuis toujours, et continueront à faire : changer la façon dont nous voyons les choses.

January 20th, 2009.

The day the country

is returned to

its rightful owner:

you.

barackobama.com

ART FOR OBAMA'S SAKE by STEVEN HELLER

The astounding amount of art created in support of Barack Obama during the 2008 presidential campaign made me think of the 19th-century French poet Théophile Gautier's term *l'art pour l'art*, "art for art's sake," to describe the essence of pure art, rather than its functional or commercial counterpart. While the images and designs aimed at getting Obama elected were not pure in Gautier's sense, arguably they are pure given the designers' honest and fervent response to this unprecedented national candidacy. The work may have been "art for Obama's sake"—it may also contain a fair share of universal signs, symbols, and even clichés—but many of the *Design for Obama* posters (and others) are as impassioned as any personal or muse-driven expression. This was not, however, the first time that artists and designers supported a presidential candidate. Given the mediocre sameness of most graphics for contemporary political campaigns, which are usually laden with patriotic clichés—red, white, and blue, stars, stripes, eagles—their unceasing redundancy has a numbing rather than rousing effect. The reason for this design rut is simple: Conventional campaign imagery is usually produced by mainstream advertising agencies slavishly following old formulas lest they make a truly novel statement that might offend a single voter.

Almost from the very beginning, the Obama campaign sought to challenge the old-school cliché-mongers with a distinctively consistent typographic graphic identity (the typeface Gotham was a nice touch), and a startling Obama "O" logo, along with Obama Blue (not quite the flag's blue, but distinctive). Yet apart from the officially sanctioned designs, the campaign received a visual energy jolt from Shepard Fairey, the Los Angeles graphic designer and street artist, who on his own dime designed a social-realist inspired portrait in blue and red with the title *Hope*. After allowing free downloads on his website, the poster seemed to post itself around the nation and in various forms throughout the world. Its viral popularity was unprecedented in American politics, but in spirit, it was not all that unique.

Artists and designers, for years, have been inspired by particular candidates and have designed posters that break the mold not only in terms of color and style but also in message and tone. Even during this campaign, a movement of grass-roots poster artists came out in droves to support Ron Paul—and some of them were effective in raising consciousness for the rogue candidate.

Independent posters may not have the same ubiquity as the sanctioned ones (Fairey's is an anomaly, although the Internet has changed the distribution paradigm and may continue to do so in the future), but they are more memorable. While not always the case, the majority of posters reject bland tropes while making novel graphic statements that reflect the times in which their candidates are running. They also target audiences that may be oblivious to the standard options. Fairey's work appeals largely to young audiences, and his poster exuded a youthful cachet.

Eventually, the Obama campaign took some ownership of the Fairey poster, and even asked him to make Obama smile; but had Fairey been "art directed" at the outset, the poster may have been even more fettered by the usual committees—or not done at all. The *The Design for Obama* artists' designs did not go through the routine vetting process; the images were unfettered by a canon and command attention because of their freshness. Arguably, not all of the images hold to the same conceptual or aesthetic standard. Some should have been art directed or never produced. But given the exceptional momentum of the Obama candidacy, and the hope that was promised, encouraging free expression was more important than design perfection.

Too many cooks, as they say, would have destroyed the immediacy of a 1968 poster for Eugene McCarthy by Ben Shahn. Rendered in his signature loose linear style, instead of a ham-fisted patriotic message, it exuded an image of hope—of change. Similarly, a poster that Andy Warhol produced in 1972—the hallmark of irony—was an impressionistic

rendering of an official portrait of Richard Nixon under which Warhol roughly scrawled "Vote McGovern." The paradox was made more poignant years later when it was revealed that Nixon's CREEP was involved with dirty tricks.

Although not my favorite, in 1996, Peter Max, who gave signed copies of his Statue of Liberty prints to whichever president was in office, created a poster for Bill Clinton and Al Gore's re-election campaign. Mr. Max's post-psychedelic poster was a youth-directed alternative to the status quo methods that define campaign graphic inertia.

Granted, breaking from firmly held traditions of American official symbolism does not add votes to a candidate's column (maybe it even takes away in some quarters), but alternative graphic approaches are decidedly more eye-catching and can only have a positive public impact. Posters, banners, and buttons are not going to sway a voter, but they may touch responsive chords with those who have already made choices. They may also redirect attention, if only for an instant—yet, that instant could be all the time needed to wrest action from the jaws of indecision.

During the McCarthy campaign, I hung the Ben Shahn poster in my apartment window. I was not just showing support for the candidate, but allying myself with my generation, which the poster's artful graphics aptly telegraphed. The Obama poster, despite the subsequent controversy over whose image was used—right or wrong—for the image, served its constituency well. When it was street art, it was a kind of pure expression (not exactly l'art pour l'art, but close) that signaled a message directly to youth culture. Even for older voters it signaled change.

The *The Design for Obama* posters did that and more. They enabled the artists and designers a chance to take part in the electoral process, to make their feelings known, and perhaps even impact others. At the very least, the myriad of posters produced for this campaign proved that if candidates' messages are not so for-mulaic, the perception of business as usual might be moot.

KUNST FÜR OBAMA von STEVEN HELLER

Die erstaunliche Menge an Kunst und Illustrationen, die im Laufe des Präsidentschaftswahlkampfs 2008 zur Unterstützung Barack Obamas geschaffen wurde, ließ mich an den Ausdruck *l'art pour l'art* denken, „die Kunst um der Kunst willen". So beschrieb der französische Dichter Théophile Gautier im 19. Jahrhundert das Wesen der reinen Kunst und bezog sich dabei weniger auf ihren funktionalen oder kommerziellen Aspekt. Die Bilder und Grafiken, die mit der Absicht entstanden, Obama zum Sieg zu verhelfen, waren sicherlich keine „reine Kunst" im Sinne Gautiers; aber man kann vielleicht in anderer Hinsicht von „Reinheit" sprechen, wenn man an die Aufrichtigkeit und den Feuereifer denkt, mit dem die Designer auf diesen außergewöhnlichen Bewerber um das Präsidentschaftsamt reagierten. Diese Arbeiten mögen „Kunst für Obama" gewesen sein – sie mögen auch einen beträchtlichen Anteil an universalen Zeichen, Symbolen und sogar Klischees enthalten –, doch viele der im Rahmen von *Design for Obama* entstandenen Plakate (und viele andere auch) sind von nicht minder großer Leidenschaft geprägt als jede persönliche oder von den Musen inspirierte künstlerische Ausdrucksform. Es war übrigens nicht das erste Mal, dass Künstler und Designer einen amerikanischen Präsidentschaftskandidaten unterstützt haben. Angesichts der immer gleichen Mittelmäßigkeit in der grafischen Gestaltung fast aller aktuellen politischen Kampagnen, die meist mit patriotischen Klischees überladen sind – Rot, Weiß, Blau, Sterne, Streifen, Adler –, hat diese nie nachlassende Redundanz einen eher betäubenden als mitreißenden Effekt. Die mangelnde Bereitschaft im Design ausgetretene Pfade zu verlassen, hat einen einfachen Grund: Das herkömmliche Grafikmaterial für Wahlkämpfe wird von etablierten Werbeagenturen erstellt, die sich sklavisch an altbewährte Formeln halten – bloß kein wahrhaft neues Statement wagen, mit dem auch nur ein einziger Wähler abgeschreckt werden könnte.

Quasi von Anfang an war die Obama-Kampagne darauf bedacht, die Klischeeproduzenten vom alten Schlage mit einer auffallend konsistenten typografischen Identität (der Font Gotham war eine gute Idee) und einem verblüffenden Obama-„O"-Logo in Verbindung mit dem Obama-Blau (es ist markant und weicht ein wenig vom Blau der US-Flagge ab) herauszufordern. Neben dem offiziell abgesegneten Design erhielt die Kampagne eine visuelle Energiespritze von Shepard Fairey, dem Grafiker und Streetart-Künstler aus Los Angeles, der aus eigenem Antrieb ein vom sozialen Realismus inspiriertes Obama-Porträt in Blau und Rot mit dem Titel *Hope* entwarf. Nachdem er das Poster als kostenlosen Download auf seiner Website zur Ver-

fügung gestellt hatte, wurde es in den Vereinigten Staaten und in gewisser Weise rund um den Globus zum Selbstläufer. Diese Art des viralen Marketing hatte in der amerikanischen Politik noch nie ihresgleichen erlebt, doch die Idee hinter dem Plakat war nicht ganz neu.

Künstler und Designer haben sich seit vielen Jahren von bestimmten politischen Kandidaten inspirieren lassen und Plakate entworfen, die von der Norm abweichen, nicht nur in Farb- und Stilgebung, sondern auch in Ton und Aussage. Während des Wahlkampfs 2008 gab es auch eine Bewegung von selbst organisierten Plakatkünstlern, die zuhauf Ron Paul

unterstützten – und einige hatten durchaus Erfolg damit und machten auf den Außenseiterkandidaten aufmerksam.

Inoffizielle Plakate mögen nicht so weite Verbreitung finden wie die offiziellen (Faireys Plakat ist eine Ausnahme, allerdings haben sich die Distributionskanäle durch das Internet stark verändert und werden sich auch in Zukunft weiter verändern), aber sie bleiben besser im Gedächtnis. Nicht alle, aber eine Mehrheit der Poster wendet sich ab von abgeschmackten Klischees und trifft neuartige grafische Aussagen, die einen Bezug zu der Zeit haben, in der sich die Kandidaten zur Wahl stellen. Ihr Zielpublikum würdigt die offiziellen Politplakate mit ihren Standardlösungen in der Regel keines Blickes. Faireys Werk strahlt Jugendlichkeit aus und spricht vornehmlich junge Leute an.

Im Laufe der Zeit wurde das Fairey-Plakat in die offizielle Obama-Kampagne integriert und Fairey wurde sogar gebeten, ob er Obama nicht lächeln lassen könnte. Wenn Fairey aber von vornherein Vorgaben eines Artdirectors gehabt hätte, wäre das Plakat wahrscheinlich von den üblichen Komitees noch weiter geglättet worden – oder gar nicht erst entstanden. Die Entwürfe, die für *Design for Obama* angefertigt wurden, brauchten die routinemäßigen Sicherheitsüberprüfungen nicht zu durchlaufen, die Bilder mussten sich nicht an den üblichen Richtlinien orientieren und fordern durch ihre Frische Aufmerksamkeit ein. Es mag sein, dass nicht alle Bilder dieselben konzeptionellen oder ästhetischen Standards erfüllen. Einige hätten einer kreativen Führung bedurft oder hätten einer offiziellen Produktion nicht standgehalten. Doch angesichts der beispiellosen Dynamik der Obama-Kandidatur und der von ihm personifizierten Hoffnung war die Ermutigung zu freiem Ausdruck wichtiger als ein perfektes Designergebnis.

Viele Köche verderben den Brei, wie man sagt, und hätten auch der Unmittelbarkeit des Plakats im Wege gestanden, das Ben Shahn 1968 für Eugene McCarthy entwarf. Es war im für ihn typischen Stil locker gezeichnet, und statt einer bedeutungsschweren patriotischen

polar bears for obama

Sentenz vermittelte es ein Bild der Hoffnung – der Veränderung. In ähnlicher Weise – allerdings mit unverhohlener Ironie – benutzte Andy Warhol 1972 für ein Poster ein offizielles Richard-Nixon-Porträt, das er impressionistisch verfremdete und unter das er „Wählt McGovern" kritzelte. Der Sarkasmus sollte sich Jahre später als äußerst angemessen erweisen, als sich herausstellte, mit welch schmutzigen Tricks bei Nixons Kampagne zur Wiederwahl gearbeitet wurde.

1996 entwarf Peter Max, der allerdings nicht zu meinen Favoriten zählt und jedem im Amt befindlichen Präsidenten signierte Exemplare seines Freiheitsstatuen-Posters schenkte, ein Plakat für die Kampagne zur Wiederwahl von Bill Clinton und Al Gore. Max' postpsychedelisches Poster war eine an die Jugend gerichtete Alternative zu den Methoden der bleischweren Wahlkampfgrafiken.

Es ist natürlich wahr, dass die Abkehr von der hehren Tradition der offiziellen amerikanischen Symbolsprache einem Kandidaten nicht unbedingt mehr Stimmen beschert (vielleicht bringt sie ihm in manchen Lagern sogar Verluste ein), doch alternative Ansätze fallen viel stärker ins Auge und können insgesamt nur eine positive Wirkung auf die Öffentlichkeit ausüben. Plakate, Aufkleber und Buttons werden keinen Wähler umstimmen, aber sie können vielleicht bei denen eine Saite anschlagen, die ihre Wahl schon getroffen haben. Vielleicht lenken sie die Aufmerksamkeit auf sich, wenn auch nur für einen kurzen Augenblick – aber vielleicht ist es ja genau jener Augenblick, der entscheidend ist, um aus der Unentschlossenheit eine Handlung werden zu lassen.

Als Eugene McCarthy für das Präsidentschaftsamt kandidierte, hängte ich das Ben-Shahn-Poster in meiner Wohnung ins Fenster. Ich wollte nicht nur meine politische Meinung kundtun, sondern mich als Teil meiner Generation zeigen, die in der künstlerischen Grafik so pointiert zum Ausdruck kam. Das Obama-Plakat leistete seiner potenziellen Wählerschaft gute Dienste, trotz der späteren Auseinandersetzung darüber, wessen Foto

– zu Recht oder zu Unrecht – als Vorlage benutzt worden war. Als Streetart stellte es eine Art reinen Ausdruck dar (vielleicht nicht unmittelbar im Sinne von *l'art pour l'art*, aber in einem ähnlichen Sinne), der die Jugendkultur mit seiner Botschaft direkt ansprach. Für ältere Wähler signalisierte dieses Plakat zumindest Veränderung.

Das und noch viel mehr ist das Werk der *Design for Obama*-Plakate. Zeichnern und

Grafikern wurde eine Gelegenheit gegeben, am demokratischen Prozess teilzunehmen, ihren Gefühlen Ausdruck zu verleihen und vielleicht sogar andere damit zu erreichen. Zumindest bewies die Unzahl von Plakaten, die für diesen Kandidaten produziert wurden, dass auch der Wahlkampf nicht mehr seinen gewohnten Gang nimmt, wenn die Aussagen eines Politikers weniger abgedroschen als gewohnt sind.

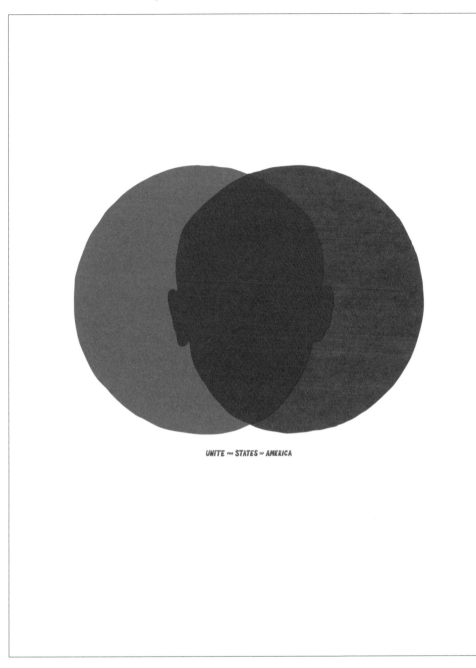

UNITE ᵗʰᵉ STATES ᵒᶠ AMERICA

la première fois que les artistes et designers soutiennent un candidat à la présidence. Étant données la médiocrité et la banalité de la plupart des créations graphiques dont accouchent les partis politiques contemporains, généralement chargés de clichés patriotiques – le rouge, le blanc et le bleu, les étoiles, les rayures, les aigles –, leur caractère redondant a un effet plus soporifique qu'enthousiasmant. La raison de cette iconographie routinière est simple : le matériel de campagne des grands partis est généralement conçu par des agences de publicité conservatrices qui suivent aveuglément les vieilles formules pour ne surtout pas risquer de choquer l'électeur par un message trop novateur.

Quasiment depuis le début, la campagne d'Obama a cherché à défier les habitudes de l'ancienne école moutonnière et élaboré une identité graphique et typographique cohérente : la police de caractères Gotham (un excellent choix), un beau logo accentuant le O de Obama, et le bleu Obama (pas exactement celui du drapeau). Pourtant, en plus de ces visuels officiellement approuvés, la campagne a reçu un électrochoc décisif grâce à Shepard Fairey, graphiste et artiste de rue de Los Angeles, qui a créé, de sa propre initiative et sans demander un sou, un portrait d'inspiration sociale-réaliste en bleu et rouge arborant le mot *Hope*. Il a autorisé son téléchargement gratuit sur son site et l'image a commencé à circuler comme par magie et sous des formes diverses, dans tout le pays puis dans le monde entier. Par son ampleur, cette popularité « virale » est sans précédent dans l'histoire politique américaine mais, dans l'esprit, elle n'est pas si unique que cela.

Depuis des années déjà, artistes et designers s'inspirent d'un candidat ou d'un autre pour créer des affiches qui brisent le moule non seulement par le choix de couleurs ou le style, mais aussi par le message et le ton employé. Au cours de cette même campagne, d'autres artistes en herbe ont œuvré pour Ron Paul – et certains ont réussi à faire connaître davantage le candidat libertaire.

Les affiches indépendantes ne sont peut-être pas aussi consensuelles que les outils de

L'invraisemblable quantité d'œuvres d'art créées pour soutenir Barack Obama pendant la campagne présidentielle de 2008 m'a fait penser au poète français du 19ᵉ siècle Théophile Gautier et à son mouvement de *L'art pour l'art*, dont l'ambition était de révéler la quintessence de l'art plutôt que son caractère fonctionnel ou commercial. Ces images et graphismes, créés pour faire élire Obama, ne répondent sans doute pas aux critères de Gautier, mais ils n'en

sont pas moins purs, puisqu'il s'agit de la réaction sincère et fervente de créateurs à cette candidature sans précédent dans l'histoire. Leur œuvre est peut-être le fruit de « l'art pour Obama » – elle contient sans doute aussi un grand nombre de signes et de symboles universels, de clichés, même –, mais une bonne partie des affiches de *Design for Obama* (et d'autres) expriment autant de passion qu'une œuvre personnelle inspirée par les muses. Ce n'est pas promotion politique officiels (celle de Fairey est une anomalie, même si Internet a radicalement changé la donne en matière de distribution et continuera à le faire dans l'avenir), mais elles sont plus mémorables. Même si ce n'est pas toujours le cas, la majorité des affiches rejettent le vocabulaire conventionnel, fade, au profit de prises de position graphiques novatrices qui reflètent l'époque dans laquelle les candidats s'inscrivent. Elles ciblent aussi un public peu touché par les moyens de promotion traditionnels. Le travail de Fairey s'adresse principalement aux jeunes, et son portrait est imprégné de références à la culture jeune.

patriotique maladroit, mais une image imprégnée d'espoir, de changement. En 1972, Andy Warhol reprend un portrait officiel de Richard Nixon, sous lequel ce maître de l'ironie griffonne «Votez McGovern». Le paradoxe est apparu de façon plus frappante encore quand le grand public a appris, quelques années plus tard, que le Comité pour la réélection de Nixon était impliqué dans des affaires louches.

Même si je n'apprécie pas particulièrement son travail, Peter Max, qui a envoyé des exemplaires dédicacés de sa statue de la Liberté aux présidents successifs, a réalisé en 1996 une affiche pour la réélection du tandem

pas un électeur, mais elles pourront toucher la corde sensible de ceux qui ont déjà fait leur choix. Elles pourront aussi attirer l'attention, ne serait-ce qu'un instant – mais un instant qui pourrait suffire à faire bondir un électeur hors des sables mouvants de l'indécision.

Pendant la campagne de McCarthy, j'ai accroché l'affiche de Ben Shahn à la fenêtre de mon appartement. Par ce geste, je ne me contentais pas de montrer mon soutien au candidat, je m'alliais aussi à ma génération, qui s'exprimait dans ce style ludique. L'affiche pour Obama, malgré la polémique qu'elle a déclenchée, fondée ou pas, a admirablement

Les responsables de la campagne d'Obama se sont finalement saisi de l'image de Fairey, et lui ont même demandé de faire sourire Obama; si Fairey avait été ainsi «aiguillé» dès le départ, l'affiche aurait probablement été entravée par les clichés habituels – ou n'aurait pas existé du tout. Les artistes dont les créations sont présentées dans *Design for Obama* sont libres de toute entrave et c'est cette fraîcheur qui attire et retient l'attention.

Trop de cuisine, comme ils disent, aurait détruit l'impact de l'affiche sur Eugene McCarthy conçue en 1968 par Ben Shahn. Réalisée dans le style relâché et linéaire qui est sa marque, elle met en avant non un message

Bill Clinton-Al Gore. L'affiche post-psychédélique de M. Max était alors aussi une alternative moderne aux méthodes de communication conventionnelles qui entretiennent l'inertie du graphisme politique.

Il est bien évident que la rupture avec les traditions profondément ancrées du symbolisme américain officiel ne garantit pas l'obtention de suffrages supplémentaires (peut-être même dissuade-t-elle quelques électeurs dans certains quartiers), mais les approches graphiques non-conventionnelles sont sans conteste plus accrocheuses et ne peuvent avoir qu'un impact positif sur le public. Les affiches, les banderoles et les badges ne convaincront

servi sa cause. Art de la rue, l'image était du domaine de l'expression libre, un message directement adressé à la jeunesse de ces rues. Les électeurs plus âgés y ont aussi lu le changement.

Les affiches de *Design for Obama* ont accompli tout cela. Elles ont permis à des artistes et à des designers de participer au processus électoral, de communiquer leurs impressions, et peut-être même d'influencer la population. Le moins qu'on puisse dire, c'est que la myriade d'affiches produites pour cette campagne a démontré que, si les messages des candidats deviennent moins stéréotypés, la perception routinière de la politique n'est pas une fatalité.

Obama'08

Al
Co
To

rs
ether.

POSTERS

WWW.**BARACKOBAMA**.COM

Obama'08
BarackObama.com

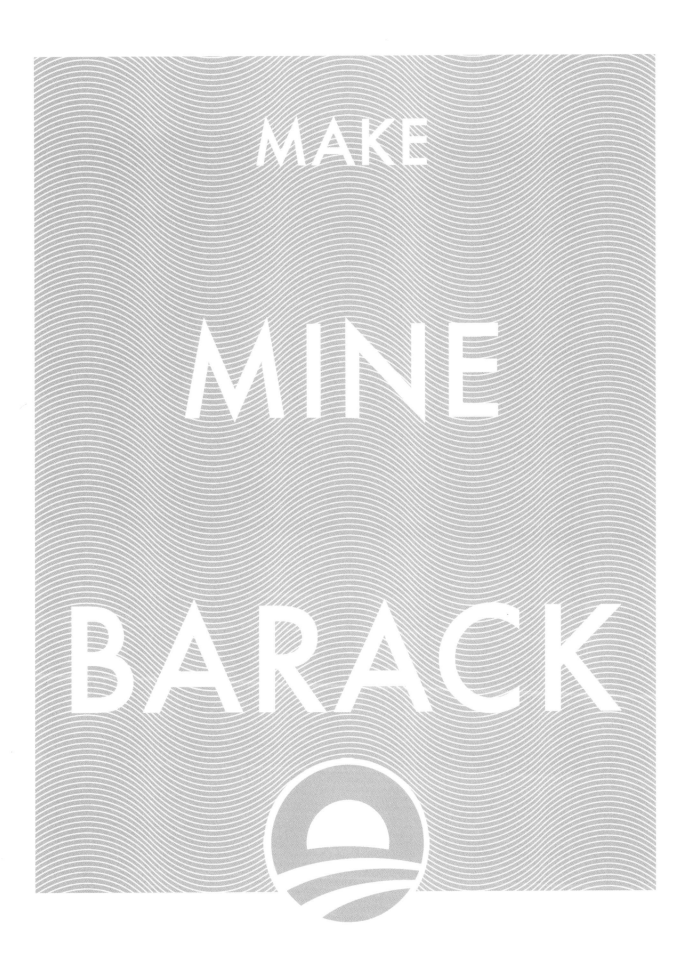

WORKING FAMILIES FOR OBAMA OBAMA FOR WORKING FAMILIES

UNTITLED by PATRICK GALLO and MIKE PINTAR

CHANGE

O8BAMA by CAREN LITHERLAND   opposite: **A NEW WORLD IS NOW POSSIBLE** by PABLO REYES PIZARRO

A NEW WORLD IS NOW POSSIBLE

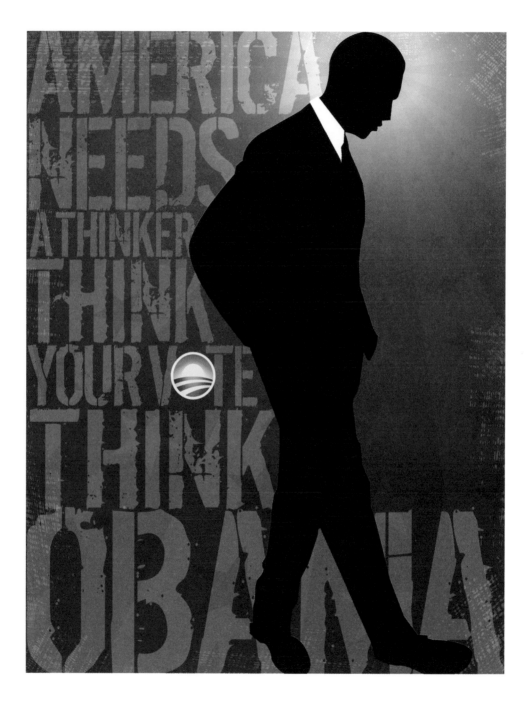

AMERICA NEEDS A THINKER by GLENNYS ANGLADA   opposite: **BARACK OBAMA: MAKING WAVES** by JAMES D. NESBITT

OBAMA'08
WWW.BARACKOBAMA.COM

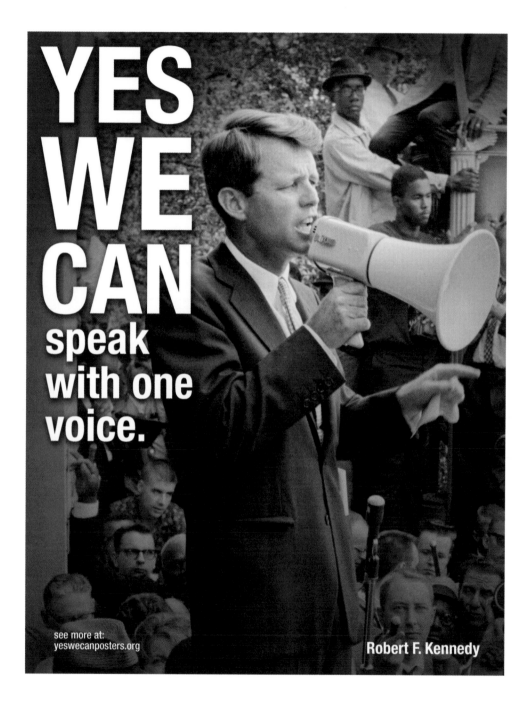

YES WE CAN speak with one voice.

see more at:
yeswecanposters.org

Robert F. Kennedy

VOTE
AND
LIVE!

CHANGEWENEED
OBAMA 2008

YES WE CAN
OBAMA
THIS IS OUR MOMENT
WHEN WE BEGIN TO PROVIDE CARE FOR THE SICK
GOOD JOBS TO THE JOBLESS
WHEN THE RISE OF THE OCEANS BEGINS TO SLOW
AND OUR PLANET BEGINS TO HEAL
WHEN WE END A WAR
SECURE OUR NATION AND RESTORE OUR IMAGE
AS THE LAST BEST HOPE ON EARTH
WE COME TOGETHER NOW

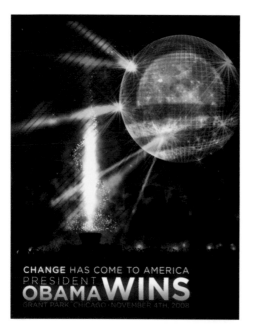

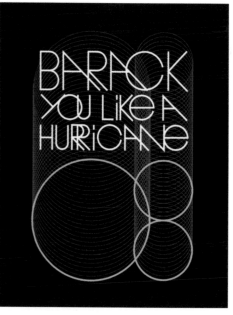

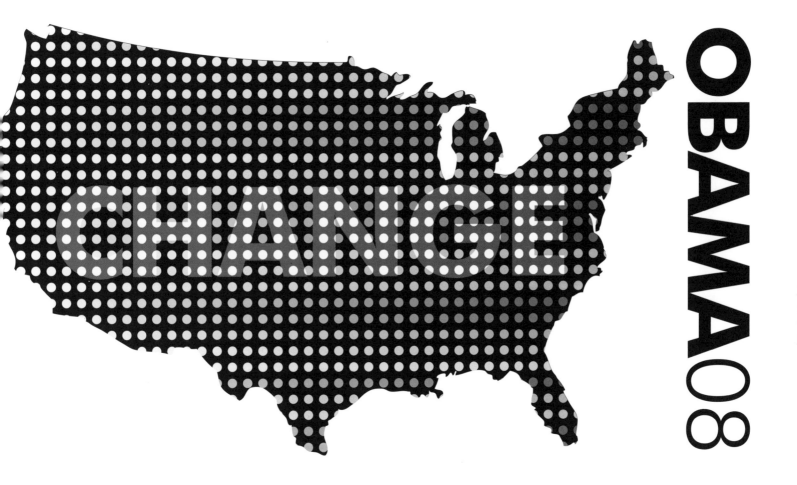

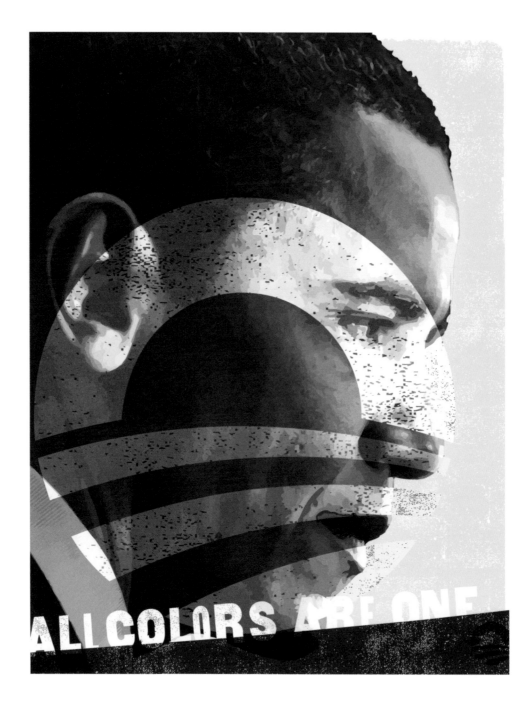

ALL COLORS ARE ONE by RYAN BYRD   previous: PROGRESSIVE SATURATION by BRIAN W. FRASER

Obama/Biden/2008
www.barackobama.com

REGULATE
THE BANKS
NOT
OUR BODIES

VOTE
OBAMA-BIDEN

one man with courage
is a majority.

i destroy my enemies
when i make them
my friends.

obama.

never bow
to the shrine of intolerance.

obama.

anyone who trades
freedom for security
deserves neither.

obama.

evil triumphs
when good men
do nothing.

obama.

IF YOU VOTE
WE GO SOMEWHERE
IF YOU DON'T
WE GO NOWHERE

ONE GIANT LEAP FOR MANKIND by XHENGIS ALIU

opposite: **A REASON TO VOTE** by GLENNYS ANGLADA

OBAMERICA by CHRISTIANO ANDREOTTI · opposite: **ALL COLORS TOGETHER** by RENAN MOLIN

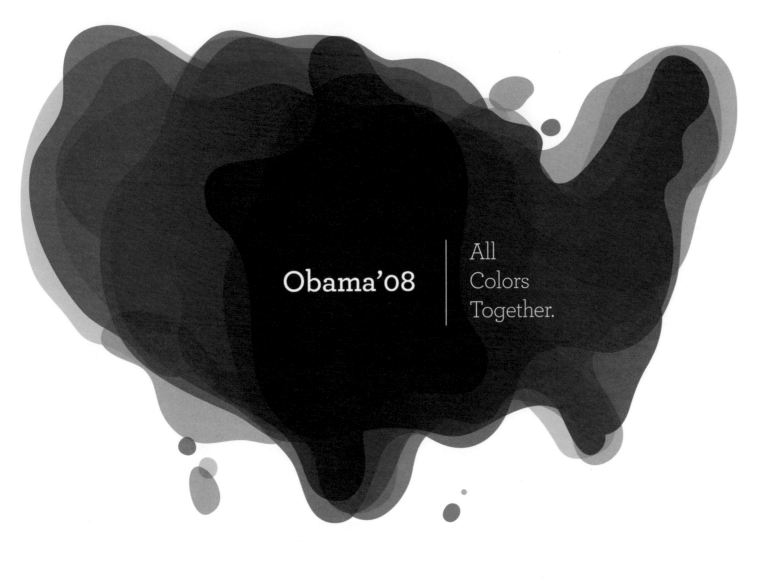

Obama'08 | All Colors Together.

VOTE! by STRAWBERRYLUNA

OBAMA'08
WWW.BARACKOBAMA.COM

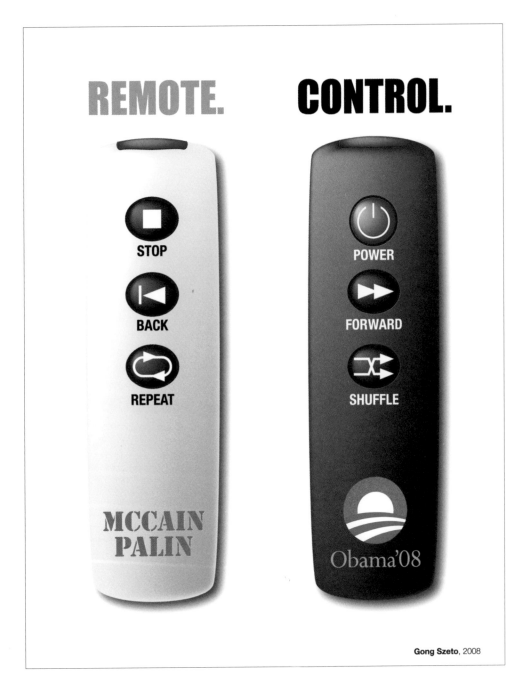

Gong Szeto, 2008

opposite: **I'M WITH THAT ONE** by CHRISTIAN PALINO

I'M WITH THAT ◯NE

OBAMABIDEN

WWW.**BARACKOBAMA**.COM

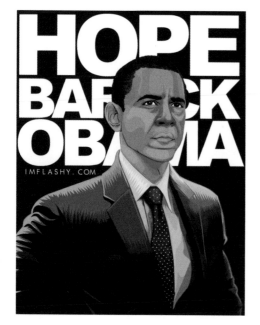

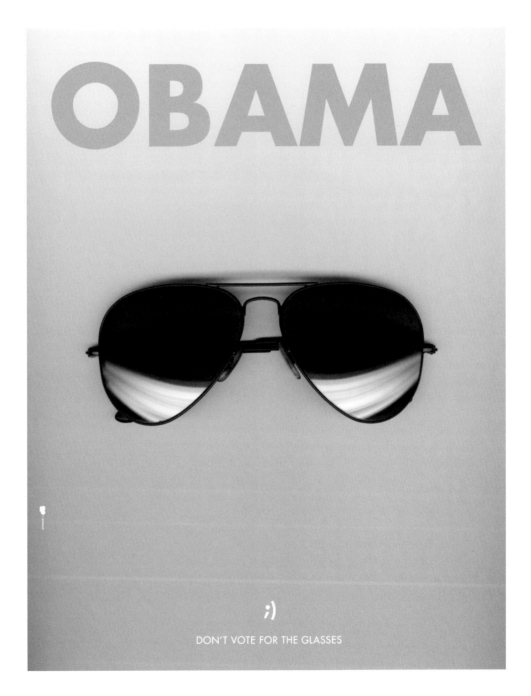

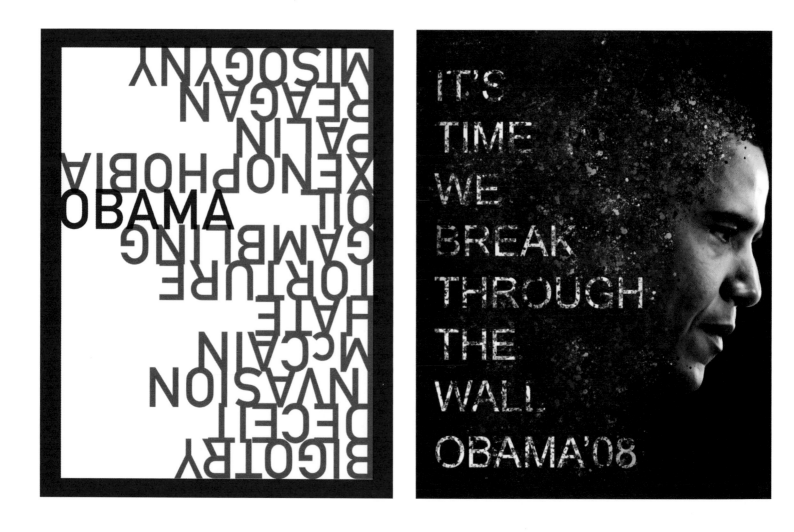

YES WE CAN by ERIC REWITZER

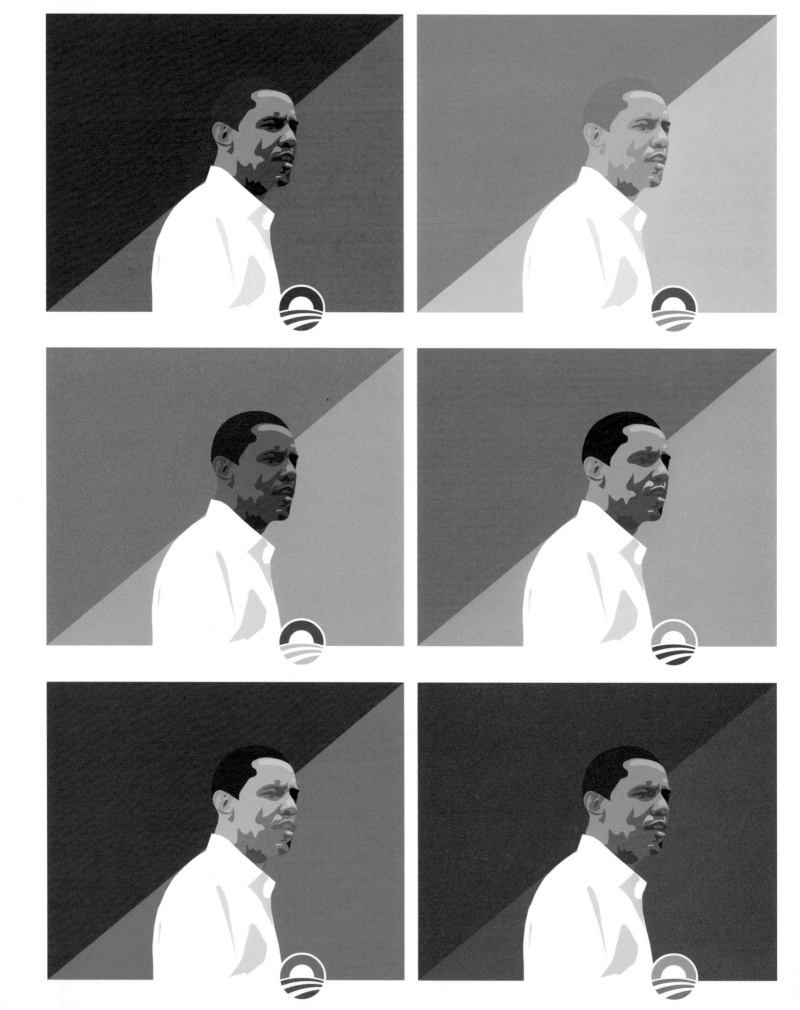

Somewhere Obama the rainbow
Skies are blue,
And the dreams that you dare to dream
Really do come true.

VICTORY by IVETTE MONTES DE OCA

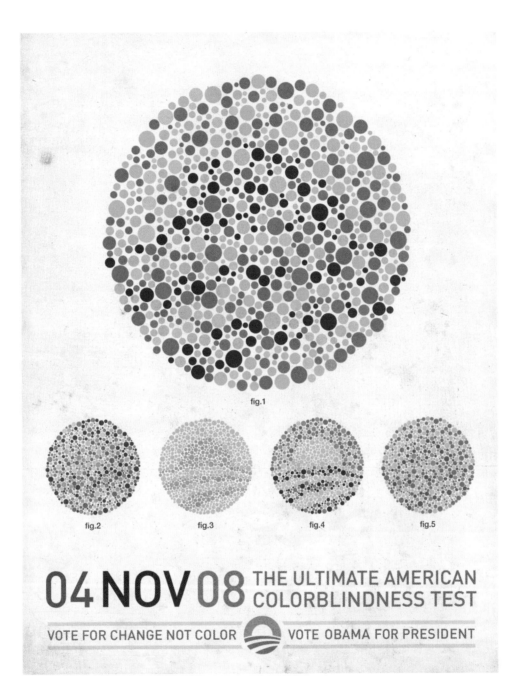

fig.1

fig.2   fig.3   fig.4   fig.5

04 NOV 08 THE ULTIMATE AMERICAN COLORBLINDNESS TEST

VOTE FOR CHANGE NOT COLOR   VOTE OBAMA FOR PRESIDENT

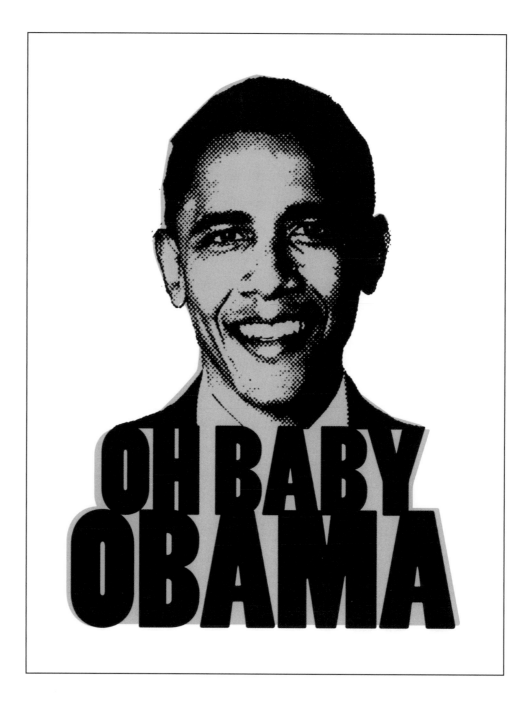

 opposite: **BABY GOT HOPE** by ROBT SEDA-SCHREIBER

THAT ONE by DARRELL J. CREDEUR

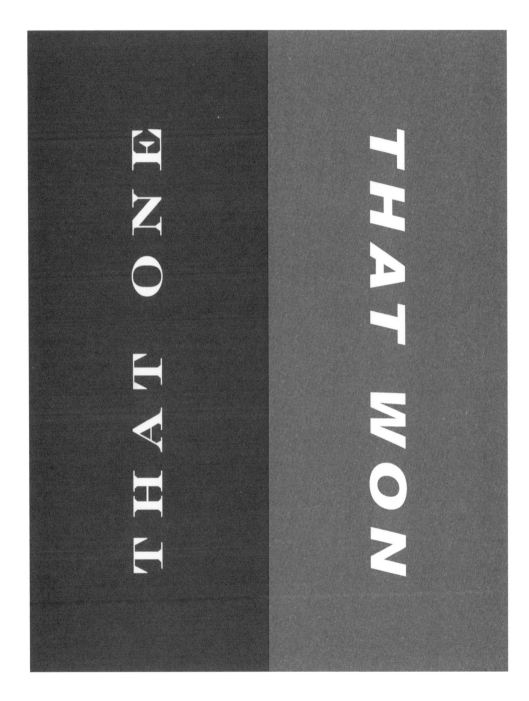

CHOOSE HOPE OVER FEAR

OBAMA BIDEN 2008

CHOOSE HOPE OVER FEAR by RICHARD PEREZ   opposite **UNTITLED** by KALEB DUROCHER

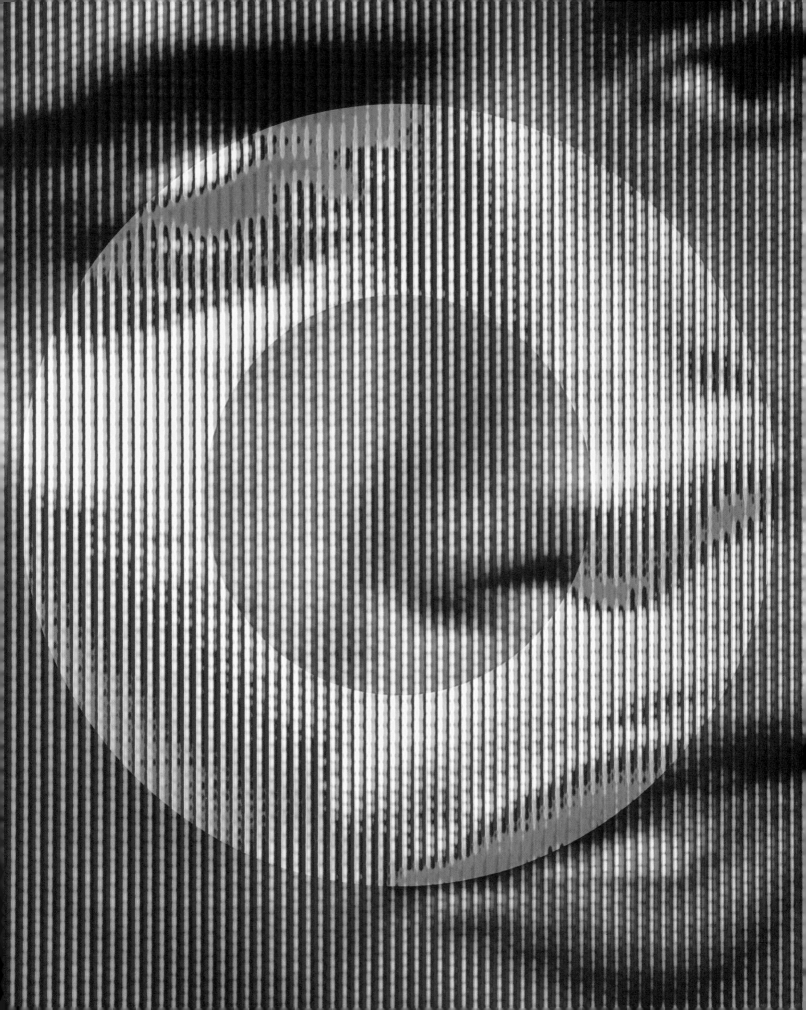

VOTE **BARACK OBAMA** / **JOE BIDEN** 2008

GOBAMA! by CHRIS PIASCIK

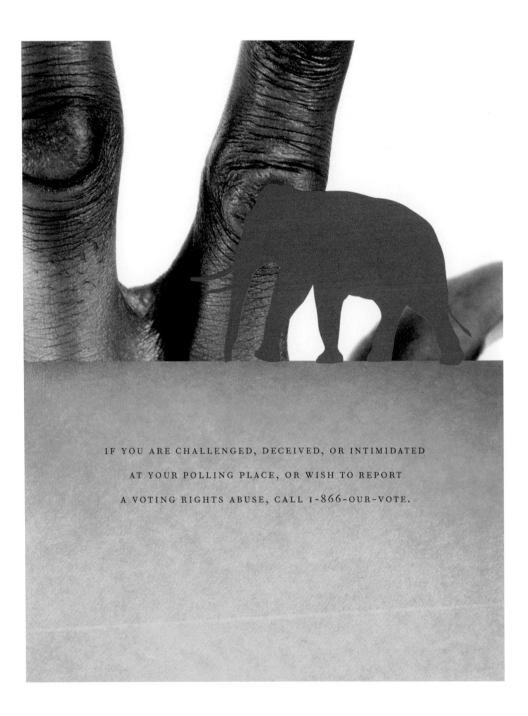

IF YOU ARE CHALLENGED, DECEIVED, OR INTIMIDATED
AT YOUR POLLING PLACE, OR WISH TO REPORT
A VOTING RIGHTS ABUSE, CALL 1-866-OUR-VOTE.

opposite: **JUST TALKIN BOUT OBAMA** by DARREN NEWBY

OBAMANOS! by MIGUEL AYUSO

DEMOCRACY, LIBERTY, OPPORTUNITY, AND UNYIELDING HOPE by KEITH WEAVER

opposite: **ONE HOUSE** by PHILIP TIDWELL

a new direction.

OBAMA 08

UNITED STATES PRESIDENT (D) ★ 2008

Obamatime

UNTITLED by JEFF CLARK

PROBAMA
NATION

THERE'S NOT A LIBERAL AMERICA AND A CONCERVATIVE AMERICA. THERE'S A UNITED STATES OF AMERICA.

CAST YOUR VOTE THIS NOVEMBER  08

STANDUP SPEAKUP08

```
C:> run hope

                        . . . .   ..
                .=OOOOOOOOOOOI .
            ..IOOOOOOOOOOOOOOOOOO8..
          ...OOOOOOOOOOBAMAOOOOOOOOO=
        . OOOOOOOOOOOOOOOOOOOOOOOOO .
        : OOOOOOOOOOOOOOOOOOOOOOOOOO$
       . OOOOOOOOOO=.       .  OOOOOOOOOO
      . OOOOOOOOO .             . IOOOOOOOOO
     . OOOOOOOOO ..              ..OOOOOOOOO.
     . OOOOOOOO .                 . OOOOOOOOO
     OOOOOOO=.                     . OOOOOOOOO~
     +OOOOOOO.                      ~OOOOOOOOO
     ?OOOOO,. . .  . ...~~~.. .   ... .OOOOO$
     . ..=OOOOOOOOOOOOOOOOOOOOOOOOO+ ...
     OOOOOOOOOOOOZ, .        . . $OOOO.
     OOOOOO .      . ...  . . ~~  ... .
     ...        . +OOOOOOOOOOOOOOOOOOOOO
         =OOOOOOOOOOOOOOO~. . .  ..
       . OOOOOOOOOOOO~.... .      . .$O:
       ..OOOOOO. ..           OOOOOOOO..
          . . .      ..OOOOOOOOOOO:.
                  ,OOOOOOOOOOOOI..
               :OOOOOOOOOOOO..


job obama begins 2009/01/20

C:> _
```

"O" CANADA by LISA KISS

four languages.
one people.
one hope.

switzerland supporting barack obama.

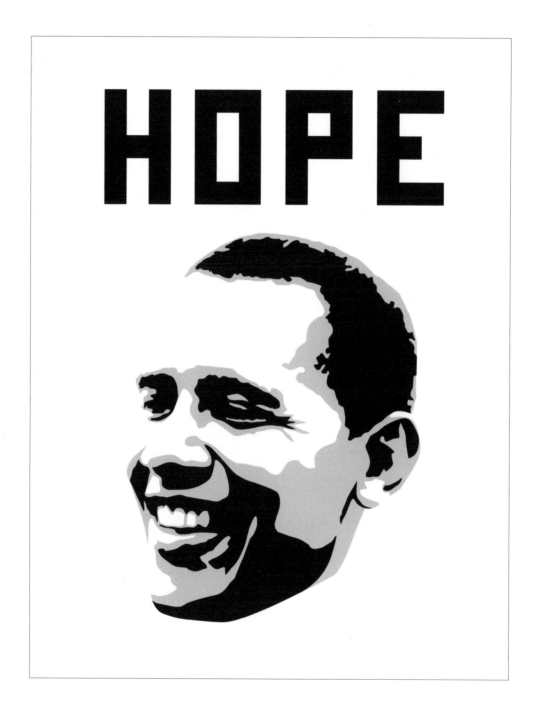

HOPE by RICHARD RODRIGUEZ   opposite: **OBAMA SILHOUETTE** by LEE ANN DOLLISON

OBAMA ◉ CHANGE

’O8AMA

YOU HAD ME AT GOTHAM by RYAN MASTALERZ

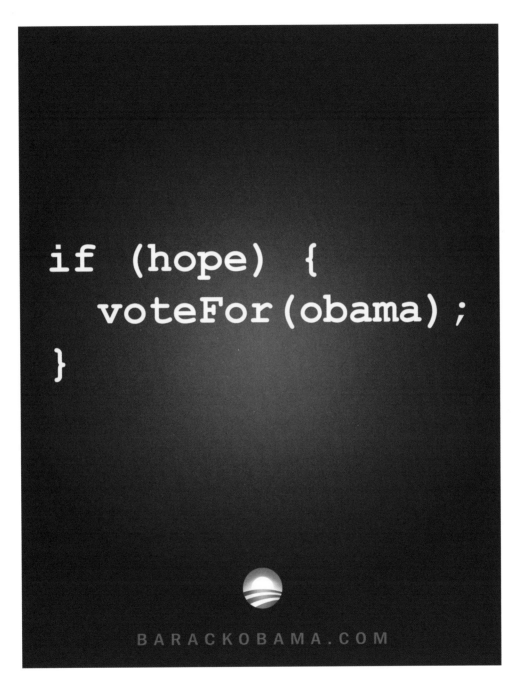

FIRED UP
CHOICES
IF THERE'S A CHILD ON THE SOUTH SIDE OF CHICAGO WHO CAN'T READ, THAT MATTERS TO ME, EVEN IF IT'S NOT MY CHILD.
GRASSROOTS
DEMOCRATIC
LOUD
WE MATTER
YOU MATTER
THE RIGHT CHOICE
HONK TO STOP THE WAR
ASSEMBLE
I PLEDGE ALLEGIANCE TO THE FLAG OF THE UNITED STATES OF AMERICA, AND TO THE UNITED
HOPE
VOTE
BARACK
THE AMERICAN DREAM
OUT OF MANY, ONE
VOICE
MY AMERICA
VOTE
HOPE
YES
WE
CAN
A CHANCE TO SUCCEED
VOTE
FREEDOM
HONESTY
YOUR AMERICA
HOPE
CHANGE
FIRED UP AND READY TO GO
DOORS OF OPPORTUNITY
GAY RIGHTS
HOPE
FAITH
IRAQ
HOPE OVER FEAR
FIX THE BROKEN WASHINGTON
CHANGE
HOPE
ONE VOICE
A CHANCE TO SUCCEED
READY TO BELIEVE
VOTE
THE ONLY WAY TO CHANGE THE WORLD IS TO PARTICIPATE AND VOTE FOR CHANGE AND HOPE
THIS IS OUR TIME
FEARLESS
CLEAN AMERICA
ONE AMERICA
VOICE
ACT
NOW
VOTE
SI SE PUEDE
IT'S OUR TIME
READY TO BELIEVE
IT'S TIME
HOPE
LOVE
VOTE
OBAMA
VOTE
VOICE
FREE SPEECH
POWER OF MILLIONS
DESIGNED BY KEVINFURSTDESIGN.COM
VOTEFORCHANGE.COM

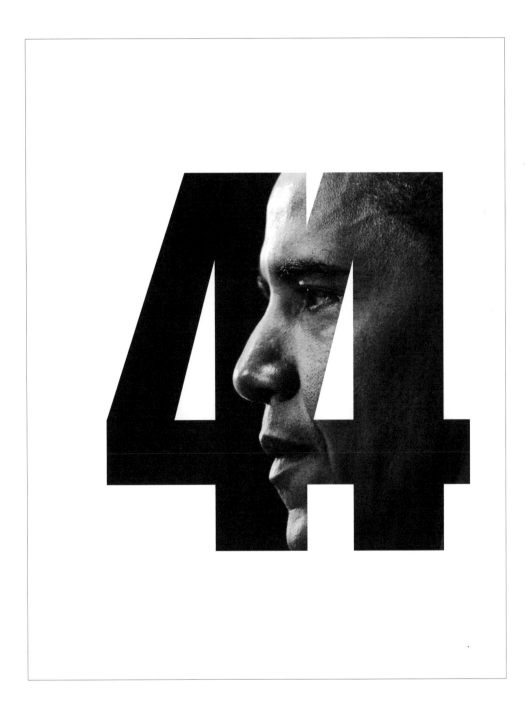

NUESTRA VOZ by RAFAEL LÓPEZ

HISTORY by DAN ALMASY

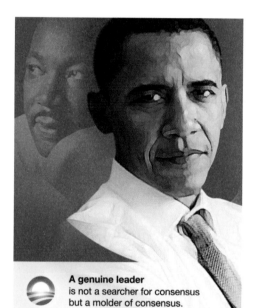

A genuine leader is not a searcher for consensus but a molder of consensus.
—Martin Luther King, Jr.

GO BAMA.

BARACK IS SAYING

ENOUGH!

TO THE LAST EIGHT YEARS

McCANT* FAILIN by CHRISTIAN PALINO

opposite: **EIGHT YEARS** by MITCHELL PHILLIPS

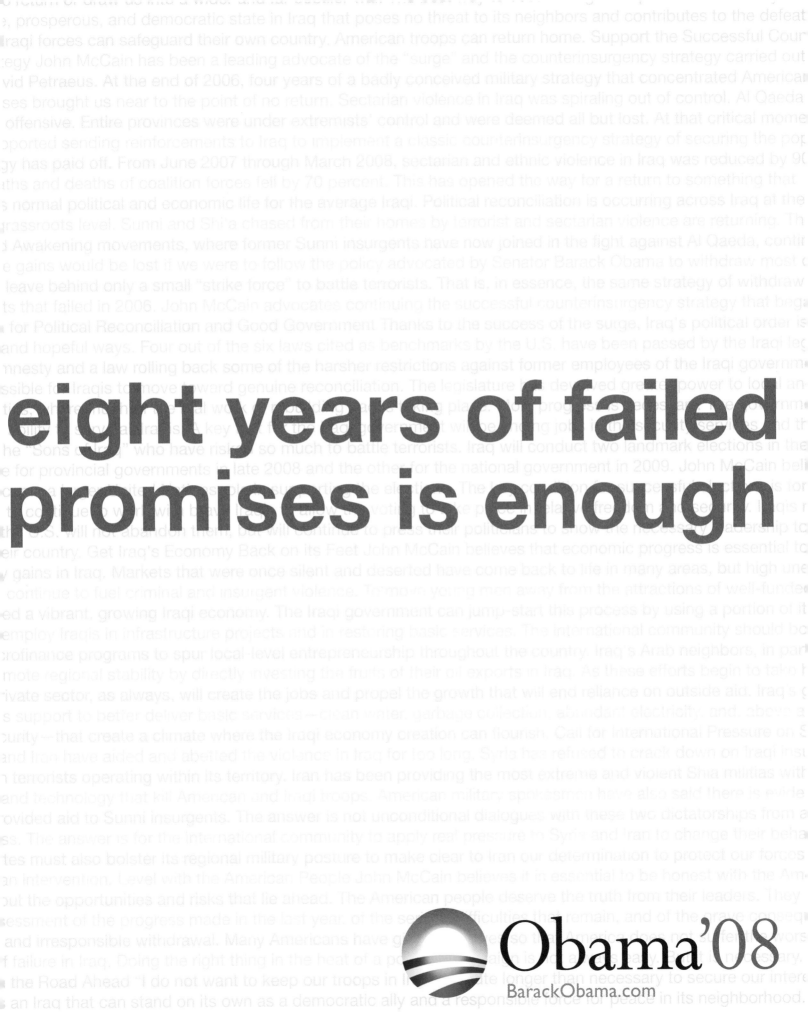

eight years of failed promises is enough

Obama '08
BarackObama.com

OBAMA,
GIVE ME
A GREEN CARD
SO I CAN VOTE.

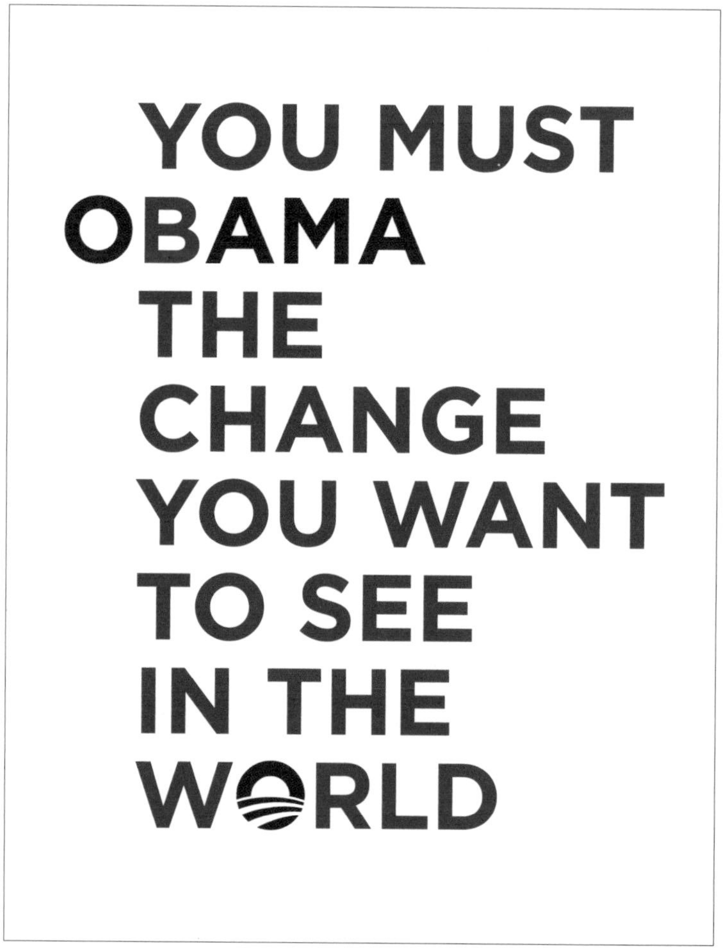

YOU MUST
OBAMA
THE
CHANGE
YOU WANT
TO SEE
IN THE
WORLD

EGNAHC
GHECNA
NGCAEH
ANHGCE
HCGENA
CHANGE

FIND REAL CHANGE IN ◉

WE HAVE BEEN WAITING FOR

HELP by YEVGENY GLADUN

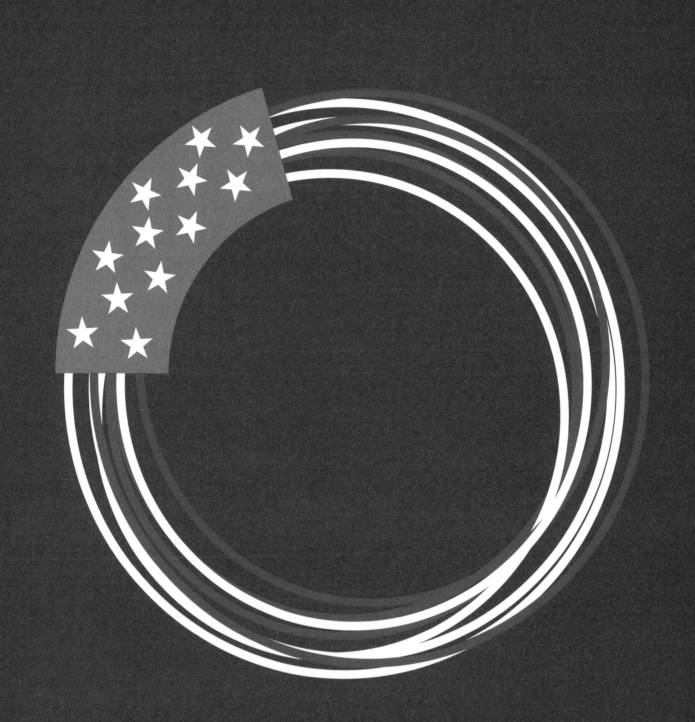

THE NEW UNITED STATES *of* AMERICA

HELPING OTHER PEOPLE EVOLVE

DESIGNERS FOR OBAMA FOR PRESIDENT

EVOLVE by ROBERT TROUTMAN

opposite: **GOBAMA** by ROBERT TROUTMAN

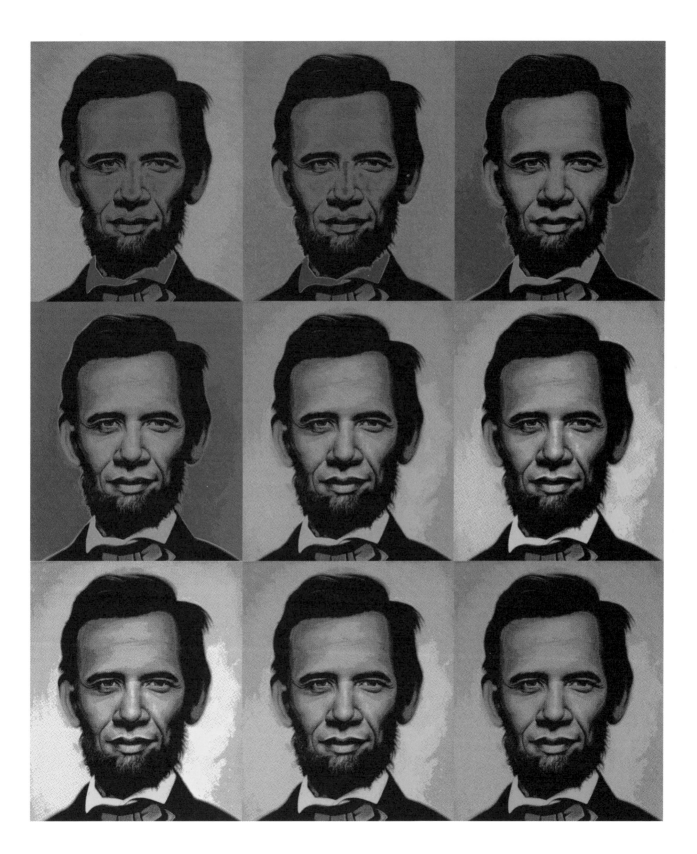

GRAPHIC DESIGNERS FOR OBAMA

>you had me at the logo.

HOPE

Obama'08

BarackObama.com

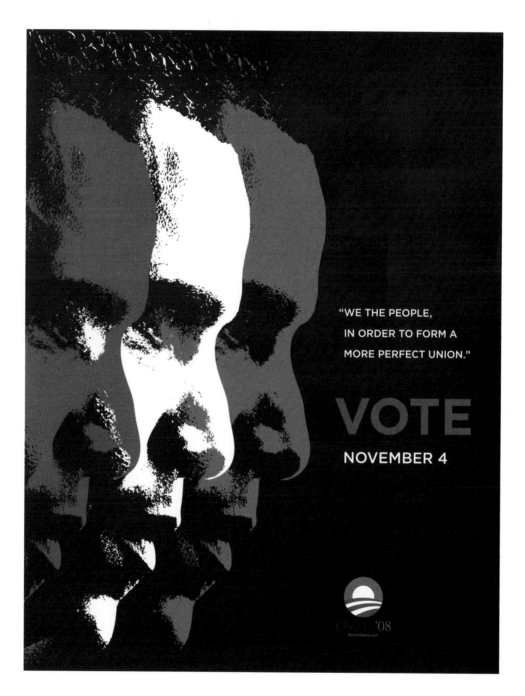

VOTE, FOR A MORE PERFECT UNION by JOHN P. FORREST JR.

FORWARD by EDDIE

opposite: **BLACK IS THE NEW PRESIDENT** by MICHAEL McMURTREY

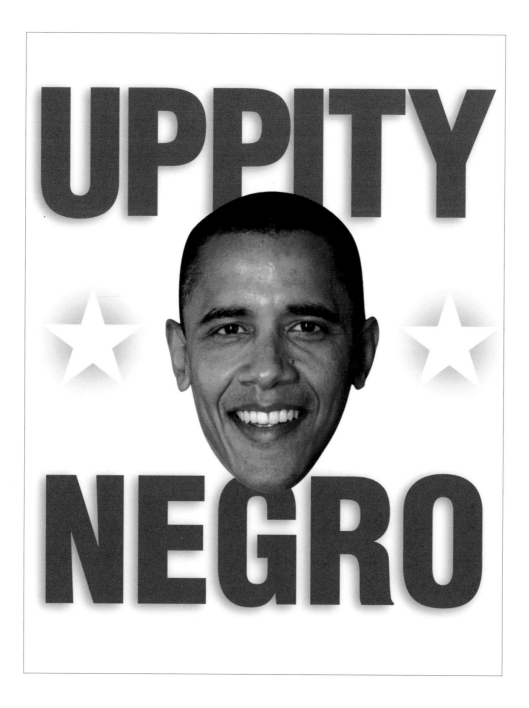

UNTITLED by JEISON RODRIGUEZ

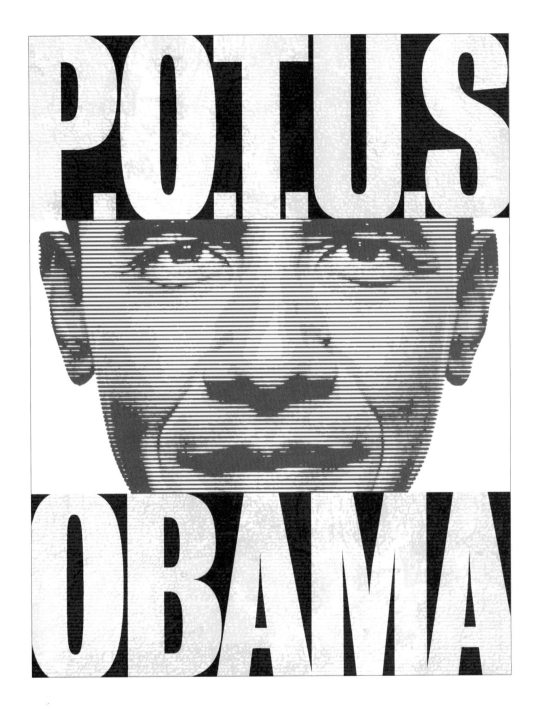

BARACK OBAMA: THE FUNKY ANSWER by ROBERLAN BORGES   opposite: **HIP HOP FOR OBAMA** by KEVIN TAYLOR and BEN GELNETT

CHANGE
WE NEED

Family values return to the White House.

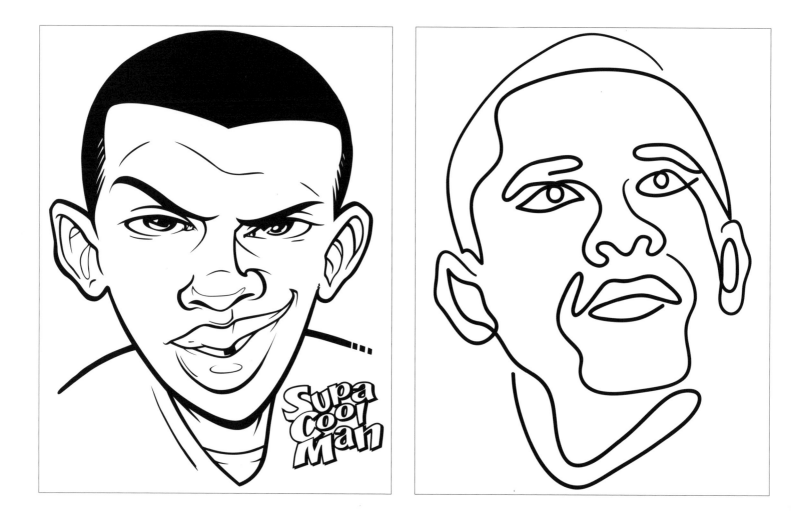

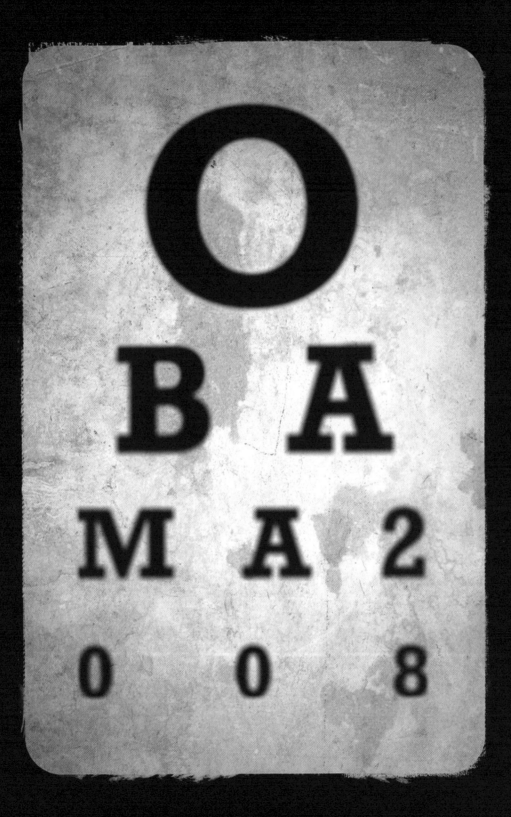

THE PEOPLE by CONSTANTINE GIAVOS

NOVEMBER 4, 2008

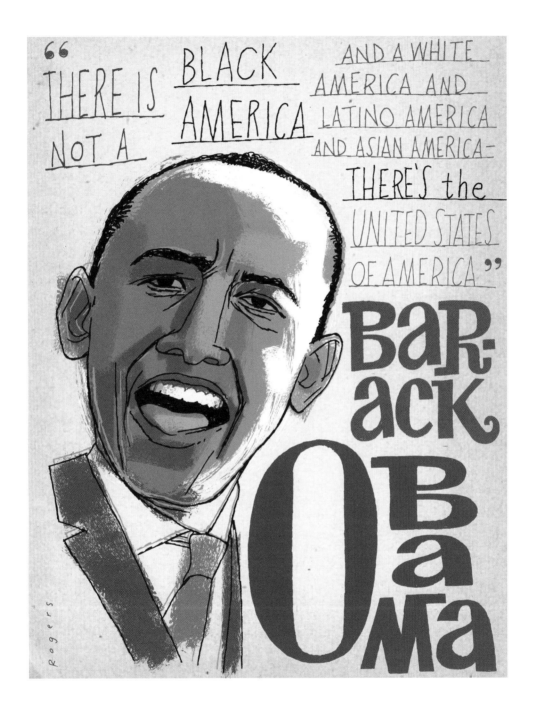

"THERE IS NOT A BLACK AMERICA AND A WHITE AMERICA AND LATINO AMERICA AND ASIAN AMERICA— THERE'S the UNITED STATES OF AMERICA"

BARACK OBAMA

Rogers

YES WE CHANGE

OBAMA 2008

A NEW DIRECTION by STUART ROCHFORD   opposite: **A MOSAIC OF PEOPLE** by CHARIS TSEVIS

POLITICS IS NOT BLACK AND WHITE

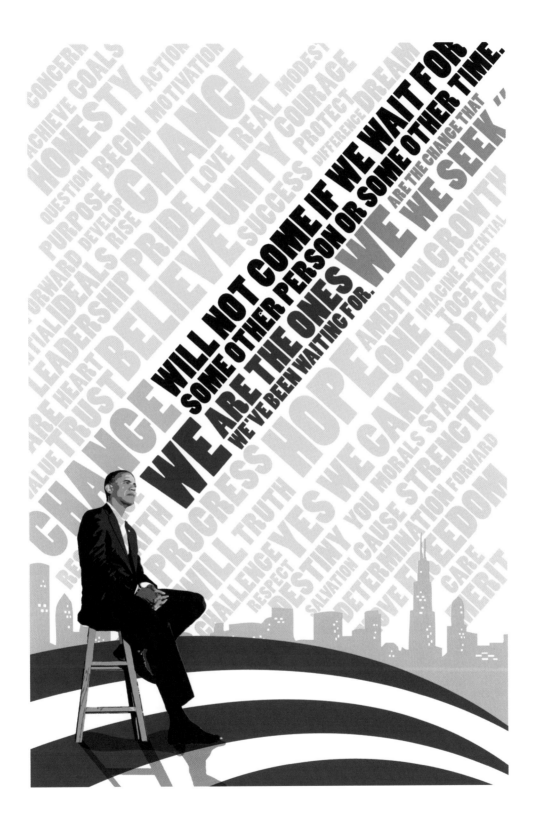

LICENSED PLUMBERS FOR OBAMA by AMOS KLAUSNER

CHANGE
WE CAN BELIEVE IN

DEE ADAMS is a contemporary artist, graphic designer, and illustrator also known as deedee9:14. She currently holds the position of senior design specialist at Yahoo! and lives in San Francisco, California.
www.deedee914.com

CRISTIANO ANDREOTTI has 20 years experience in corporate, print and packaging design with a primary focus in the creation of corporate and retail brand identity systems. He holds a BA in graphic design and marketing from Centrostudi Comunicazione in Rome.

MATTEO BALDARELLI Born in Rome, Italy, Baldarelli studied at the European Institute of Design, spent a couple of years working as a graphic designer, and now lives in London, England.
www.baldarelli.carbonmade.com

JOE ALEXANDER and **LEE DAYVAULT** A creative director at The Martin Agency in Richmond, Virginia, Joe also independently creates and directs content. Lee is a freelance art director in Atlanta who makes short viral films for the web.
www.consciencenow.blogspot.com

GLENNYS ANGLADA is a graphic designer living in Miami, Florida. He recently organized an art show honoring President Obama at an international business school in the Dominican Republic.

DAMIEN BASILE is a brand strategist for The Cause Is The Habit, which empowers businesses to be the best they can be in communications, especially in social media. He lives in Brooklyn.
www.thecauseisthehabit.com

XHENGIS ALIU is an award-winning photographer and graphic designer who recently moved from Skopje, Macedonia, to Chicago, Illinois.
http://www.xhengisaliu.com

OLIVA BERNADETTE C. ARRIOLA is a nursing student from Sun Valley, California. Raised in a culturally traditional Filipino home, her interests include biology, political science, culinary arts, and graphic design.
www.shootingasterisk.net

ROBERLAN BORGES is a Brazilian vector artist, graphic designer, and illustrator with a passion for vintage art and design. He thinks of himself as "just a guy who likes to create images."
www.roberlan.deviantart.com

DHARI AL-KHALED is a computer engineer, graphic designer, and website designer from Kuwait.

MIGUEL AYUSO Inspired by Mexican and American iconography, Ayuso's work seeks to fuse representations of both cultures, redefine notions of identity, and affect social change. He lives in Oaxaca, Mexico.
www.miguelayuso.com

DIMITRIS BORSIS is a freelance graphic designer and artist from Athens, Greece. He is a member of the band Film and has collaborated with the record label Inner Ear.
www.db-art.110mb.com

AARON ALLEN was born in Boulder, Colorado, and studied at the University of Colorado and at the Art Center College of Design in Pasadena, California. He is a creative director at Wieden and Kennedy in Portland, Oregon.

SARA BACON of Brooklyn, New York, is president and art director of Command C design, which specializes in custom web design and development, e-commerce, search engine optimization, branding, identity, and logos.
www.commandc.com

MR. BRAINWASH, a.k.a. Thierry Guetta, has documented Banksy, Shepard Fairey and others as a filmmaker. One of California's most prolific street artists, his iconic imagery is on view in New York, New York; Los Angeles, California; and Paris, France.
www.mrbrainwash.com

DAN ALMASY is a designer and photographer in Atlanta, Georgia, whose goal, at the end of the day, is to make images that people will like.
www.danalmasy.com

BRANDON BAILEY received his degree in graphic design from Nicholls State University in Thibodaux, Louisiana, where he currently works as a print and web designer.
www.bcbailey.net

NITIN BUDHIRAJA was born and raised in India, and now lives in New Haven, Connecticut, where he is a multidisciplinary graphic designer. He aims to achieve a balance of pragmatism and idealism in his life and design work.
www.dezynefactory.com

JUDE BUFFUM's work has been featured in *Graphis*, *Communication Arts*, the AIGA annual *Print*, and *American Illustration*. He teaches illustration at the University of the Arts in Philadelphia, Pennsylvania.
www.judebuffum.com

GEOFF BURKERT lives in Nashville, Tennessee, with his lovely wife and adorable toddling daughter. A record of his design pursuits can be found on his website.
www.burkertdesign.com

DON BUTTON is an award-winning graphic designer, photographer, and journalist. A former art director for *News & Review*, he is the chair of the Graphic Communication department at Sacramento City College in Sacramento, California.
www.DesignButton.com

RYAN BYRD is a husband, father, pastor, blogger, and designer from Little Rock, Arkansas. You can find him leading the faith community Eikon, spending time with his family, or grooming his frighteningly ironic facial hair.
www.beingryanbyrd.com

PAULO CARDOSO and **SUSANA FIGUEIREDO** graduated in product design from Faculdade de Arquitectura da Universidade Técnica de Lisboa in Portugal, and have collaborated on public-art, graphic-design, and product-design projects since 1998.
www.coroflot.com/cafidesign

TOM CARMONY of Bainbridge Studios is a Seattle, Washington–based designer who has been working on the web and in print since 1997. He focuses on crafting clean, intuitive design solutions for small businesses.
www.bainbridgestudios.com

BIANCA YVONNE CASIMES is a student who is driven by movement and progress, and inspired by the ability of one voice to make an impact. She lives in Seattle.
www.biancayvonne.com

SHERYL CHECKMAN is an award-winning graphic designer in New York City, with nearly 30 years experience in corporate and marketing communications.
www.checkmandesign.com

JEREMIAH CHIU and his colleagues run Plural in Chicago. With a strong focus on typography, Plural continues to create fresh visual stimuli that open the boundaries of graphic design.
www.pluralplural.com

JEFF CLARK was born in 1971 in Southern California, and lives in Ypsilanti, Michigan. For 13 years, he has made his living as a book designer and typographer. He has also published books of writing through FSG and Quemadura.
www.quemadura.net

RODRIGO CORTES As a boy, I wanted to be a painter. Later, my family moved to Mexico, where I found inspiration in the murals of Siqueiros, Rivera, and Orozco, whose art conveyed a message greater than the artwork itself.

CHRISTOPHER COX, an artist and designer, maintains the website changethethought.com, which serves as a source of daily creative inspiration for the global online design and art community. He lives in Denver, Colorado.
www.changethethought.com

DARRELL J. CREDEUR After studying art history, I was a good Cajun and worked as a roughneck on oil platforms in the Gulf of Mexico. After that dangerous job I was ready for a career in advertising.

BILL DAWSON lives and works in Los Angeles. His studio XK9 Design™ specializes in identity and motion graphics. He is a graphic designer and a progressive Democrat. "Obama 2012!"
www.xk9.com

NICK DeCARLO is a graphic designer, art director, illustrator, father, and husband currently living and working in Chicago.
www.krop.com/since75

JOHN DERRY is a pioneer of digital painting and one of the original authors of Corel Painter. He has a master's in painting from Cranbrook Academy of Art, and is a practicing artist and photographer in Omaha, Nebraska.
www.pixlart.com

LEE ANNE DOLLISON A painter from the Midwest living in sunny Santa Barbara, California, Dollison also designs textbooks. She likes to think of her designs as "practical fine art."
www.laddesign.biz

KALEB DUROCHER's work has been shown in national exhibits. He is a student in Eau Claire, Wisconsin, and art director for *NOTA*, a campus creative arts publication.
www.kalebdurocher.com

CHRISTOPHER DOUGLAS I am a furniture designer, musician, art director, and graphic designer. I created this poster because, for the first time in my adult life, I believed real change in Washington was possible.
www.lineandcurve.com

ROBERT FINKEL of Birmingham, Alabama, specializes in identity design and custom letterpress printing. He is a graduate of the Portfolio Center and holds a degree in anthropology and sociology from Rhodes College.
www.robertfinkel.com

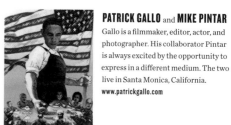

PATRICK GALLO and **MIKE PINTAR** Gallo is a filmmaker, editor, actor, and photographer. His collaborator Pintar is always excited by the opportunity to express in a different medium. The two live in Santa Monica, California.
www.patrickgallo.com

EDDIE of Oakland, California, attended the School of Visual Arts and the California College of the Arts. He believes that his public art projects, at best, are simply for initiating dialogues.
www.flickr.com/eddieicon

JOHN P. FORREST, JR., is an educator and designer. He serves as assistant professor of graphic design at California State University, Sacramento.
www.greytype.com

RENÉ GARCIA, JR., is bursting with good ideas. His art often makes people smile. He lives and loves in San Francisco.
www.renegarciajr.com

RON ENGLISH New York–based pop artist Ron English's guerilla painting pursuits have taken him from Texas to Berlin to Hong Kong. During the 2008 campaign he led a grassroots public art tour, installing "Abraham Obama" murals nationwide.
www.popaganda.com

BRIAN W. FRASER hails from Scotch Plains, New Jersey. He resides in Atlanta, where he works as a design consultant.
www.brianwfraser.com

CONSTANTINE GIAVOS is an 18-year-old Greek American from Richmond. He is a freelance designer whose clients have included *Vice* magazine and Def Jam/Island Records.
www.constantinegiavos.com

MICHAEL FABER is a designer in Durham, North Carolina. After taking a month off from work to canvass for the campaign, he created his DFO poster to try to capture the excitement of a successful election night.

FRGDR.COM Inspired by will.i.am's video and disgusted by the smear campaign, frgdr.com decided to do his part and assist Jewish Obama supporters in showing their pride in Hebrew.
www.frgdr.com

YEVGENY GLADUN was born in the USSR and studied design at RISD. He now lives in Germany, where he works as a designer and devotes his free time to photography and other artistic pursuits.
www.yevglad.com

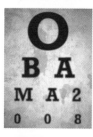

MICHELLE FARKOUH is a Brooklyn–based illustrator and graphic designer.
www.michellefarkouh.com

AMADÉ FRIES As a Swiss citizen and especially as a student of international relations, I share President Obama's strong belief in democracy. I just couldn't resist designing a poster for this campaign.
www.amade.ch

MARISTELLA GONZALEZ is a graphic designer from the Republic of Panama. She received her BFA from Savannah College of Art and Design in 2006, and is pursuing graduate studies at Pratt Institute in New York.
www.maristellagonzalez.com

COREY FAVOR is a senior graphic designer at Who's Who Publishing in Columbus, Ohio. Currently, he is preparing to launch a company that specializes in design and full-color printing.
www.nycfave.com

KEVIN J. FURST is a self-motivated, enthusiastic designer and activist who feels it is his duty to make a significant contribution to his local and global community. He lives in Philadelphia.
www.kevinfurstdesign.com

KEVIN GORMAL Born and raised in the Midwest with a strong European influence, Gormal is a designer by nature and an artist by choice. He lives in Indianapolis, Indiana.
www.kevingormal.com

RENÉE GRAEF of Cedarburg, Wisconsin, has illustrated over 70 books for children, including the American Girl Collection's Kirsten series and many of the Little House picture books.
www.reneegraef.com

BRAD KAYAL When I was young I wanted to be in the band Twisted Sister. I ended up a designer, which was probably the better outcome, as it involves a lot less spandex and long hair doesn't really suit me.
www.bradkayal.com

LISA KISS has been a graphic designer for 15 years. Her studio, Lisa Kiss Design, has been privileged to work with some of the most innovative producers of art and culture in Canada.
www.lisakissdesign.com

ALEX GRIENDLING received his BFA from Murray State University in 2007. He now lives in Los Angeles and designs movie posters for a film advertising firm.
www.alexlikesdesign.com

RYAN KELLER Iowa. Art. Design. Music. Family. Friends. Guitars. Tattoos. Barbecues. Sunglasses. Running. Vintage cars. Golden retrievers. Autumn. Film. Laughing. Comfortable sneakers. Faded jeans.

AMOS KLAUSNER is a brand manager, design historian, and writer who, in 2008, relieved his political stress by designing and sharing partisan posters on his now defunct daily blog, Democrat By Design.

JAMES HARRISON Originally from the Piney Woods of East Texas, Harrison now resides in Dallas, where he works as a designer/artist/creative.
www.howigetdown.com

JUSTIN KEMERLING's work focuses on the specifics of place; picking a side and giving image, clarity, and distinction to specific causes; designing positively for social change.
www.justinkemerling.com

CHRISTOPHER LEAL I am 22 years old and was born in Fullerton, California. At an early age, I was introduced to the wonders of photography and graphic design. I currently attend UCLA's art program.
www.christopherleal.net

ANDY HAUCK of Minneapolis, Minnesota, received his BFA in graphic design from Iowa State University. With 10 years of design experience, the "best thing about being a creative is making two-color designs come to life."

AMMAR KESHODIA is a 16-year-old student from the United Arab Emirates. He enjoys playing video games, reading depressing poetry, and setting fire to inanimate objects with his friends.
www.harmful-poet.deviantart.com

MARK S. LEE is based in Seattle. His work ranges from brand identity design to interaction design. He holds a BFA in visual communication design from the University of Washington.
www.markslee.com

TYREKE HUNT Being born with Spinal Muscular Atrophy has been a burden but never a hindrance. I have accomplished every goal I've set—one of my proudest is receiving my BFA in 2007.
www.tyrekehunt.com

ISAIAH KING is an artist, designer, and illustrator in New York. He strives to advance the presence of a socially relevant information exchange in our public environments.
www.iking design.com

JERRY LEIBOWITZ is the creator of the animated series *The Mouse and the Monster*. He has received logo and design awards from the Art Directors Club of Los Angeles, and is an exhibiting fine artist.
www.finemess.com

BARBARA KARANT A Chicago-based photographer nationally known in art and architectural communities, Karant is committed to educating the public about the marvels of living with retired racing greyhounds.
www.karant.com

BRANDON KISH is a designer and artist from St. Joseph, Michigan, who has worked in the branding, automotive, and appliance industries.

SALVATORE LILLINI is a young Italian graphic designer traveling around Europe. He started cutting paperboards at age 21 for Leo Burnett.
www.salvatorelillini.com

CAREN LITHERLAND is a New York–based graphic designer.
www.08bama.us

RAFAEL LÓPEZ Speaking with his paintbrushes, Lopez wanted to communicate the strong connection between President Obama's message and the Latino community. He lives in San Diego, California.
www.rafaellopez.com

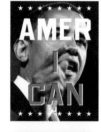

JAHRUE LYTTLE and **YAZID SHARIFF** Lyttle of Miramar, Florida, is the founder of the urban style, art, and culture blog imflashy.com. Yazid Shariff, of Malaysia, is a contributor. They collaborated on their piece, *The New Contrast.*
www.imflashy.com

CHRIS MACLEAN After five years at the British design agency The Chase, Chris traveled the world before becoming creative director of Sydney's Interbrand Australia at the age of 28.
www.chrismaclean.co.uk

PATRICK MACOMBER is a Philly designer with a dog that's afraid of cats and a cat that loves water. His gal adores him. He supports good beer and better presidents—now he has both.
www.areyounotpleased.com

RYAN MASTALERZ is a Chicago-based designer focusing on brand identity, print, and interactive media.
www.envycreative.com

PADRAIG McCOBB of Hudson, Massachusetts, is a partner and creative director at Lightning & Trumpet, which creates branded communications for a wide variety of clients across the country.
www.lightningandtrumpet.com

CHRISTOPHER McINERNEY is an illustrator and designer working out of Providence, Rhode Island.
www.craftysquid.com

BRENDAN J. McINERNEY is a free-lance photographer and designer based in the American Northeast.
www.theangrypenguin.org

KENNETH McIVER works under the name of "Esteban" and is one half of fieldsofall.com, creative graphic design and digital exploration from the north of England.
www.fieldsofall.com

MICHAEL McMURTREY is the co-founder of Design-O-Matic, which specializes in print design for clients such as Paramount, Disney, Fox, and MGM from Glendale, California, and Asheville, North Carolina.
www.designomatic.com

STEVEN MORGAN is a former Wall Street banker who has humorously chronicled his time as a transplant in New York City with "The Adventures of Supa Cool Man," a collection of webcomics and apparel.
www.57thstcomics.com

JILL MORRISON is an award-winning graphic and web designer who has been working professionally in San Francisco since 2006, mainly for small businesses, artists, and nonprofits.
www.jillmorrison.net

ADAM C. MORSE was born on the right coast. Eventually he migrated to Ohio and joined the band Ill Lillies. He now lives on the left coast, designing for Hey! Studio and playing in the band Lady Nasty.
www.heyits.us

RENAN MOLIN, a.k.a. Dmolin, works in graphic design and art direction for clients such as Pepsi, MTV, Capricho, Banco do Brasil, Oi, Tim, Editora Abril, and O Boticário. He lives in Curitiba, Paraná, Brazil.
www.dmolin.com

IVETTE MONTES DE OCA of Overlap Design, a New York studio that specializes in lifestyle brands, has a BFA from the School of Visual Arts. She has worked at Pentagram and other prominent New York firms.
www.overlapdesign.com

CHRIS MURPHY is a graphic designer, creative artist, part-time illustrator, and amateur photographer living in Kansas City, Kansas.
www.chrism70.com

JAMES D. NESBITT has been recognized by *Graphis,* Step 100, *GD, Seattle Show,* the University of Washington, and the *Prentice-Hall Reference Guide.*
www.jamesnesbittdesign.com

DARREN NEWBY is a motion and print designer/director living and working in the Midwest.
www.dnewbydesign.com

KANA OTOMO I was born in Tokyo, Japan, and now reside in New York City. Having lived in Japan, China, and the United States has enhanced my transnational perspective, which I often incorporate into my design.
www.otomokana.com

ROBBY PETRULLO is a freelance designer from Niagara Falls, Ontario. He can be found on Flickr and Smugmug under the name "toolo."
www.flickr.com/photos/toolo/

LEVI NICHOLSON Since graduating from Humber College, the Toronto, Canada–based graphic designer has earned recognition from the AIGA, ADCC, *Applied Arts*, *Communication Arts*, Coop, Good Design Awards, and *How*.
www.biohazarddesign.ca

HALLIE OVERMAN is a freelance designer in Brooklyn. Her vote was sealed after President Obama's 2004 speech at the DNC, though she admits that his love of college basketball was icing on the cake.
www.overprintinc.com

MITCHELL PHILLIPS is a creative web developer and graphic designer. He believes good design aesthetics can change the world. So…dream big and live bigger: Design something.
www.mitchellphillipsdesign.com

ANDREW J. NILSEN was raised in Akron, Ohio, and lived in France, New Zealand, and Australia before landing in San Francisco. He holds a BS in design from the University of Cincinnati and rides a unicycle.
www.andrewnilsen.com

CHRISTIAN PALINO is a design strategist at Adaptive Path in San Francisco, who has taught courses on typography and service design at IUAV University of Venice, Domus Academy, and the Interaction Design Institute Ivrea.
www.christianpalino.com

STEPHEN PHUNG is a web designer based in Vancouver, Canada.
www.stephenphung.com

LEE NORRIS As a politically aware Cleveland, Ohio–based artist and illustrator, Norris has been working on children's books, freelance art, and marketing collateral for over 10 years.
www.resume.lee-norris.com

BEKKA PALMER I decided to become a graphic designer after living in Seattle for a year. I received my education at Seattle University and afterwards moved to San Diego, where I am pursuing my passion.
www.bekka5280.com

CHRIS PIASCIK I am an artist/designer living in Cambridge, Massachusetts. I am the art director of Print Brigade, as well as a designer at Alphabet Arm. Five days a week I post drawings on my blog.
www.chrispiascik.com

GRAEME OFFORD is a New Zealand–born graphic designer living in New York.
www.graemeofford.com

CR PEARCE is a student in video production and digital art at Indiana University and an AmeriCorps alumnus. In the future he would like to work in the world of animation and cartoons.
www.wallpaperforobama.blogspot.com

ROBERT PIOTROWSKI is an expatriate architect living and working in Buchen, Germany. He is a partner at Ecker Architekten.
www.ecker-architekten.de

CHIGOZIE ORIEH is an up-and-coming graphic designer in Houston, Texas. While at a traffic light, he and his wife, Amber, assisted a homeless person with a few dollars—and the idea for this poster was born.
www.amartwerkz.com

RICHARD PEREZ is a graphic designer and illustrator from San Francisco. He loves creating posters, doodling, and making people smile. He'd be content doing something that involves all three things.
www.skinnyships.com

MATTEO POLATI is a web designer and illustrator based in Verona, Italy.
www.gongon2.com

PABLO REYES PIZARRO I'm studying graphic design in Chile; I've wanted to do this since I was a kid. My family was involved with design, so I was started very young in this world!

NICHOLAS ROCK is a graphic designer living and working in Rhode Island. He is a recent graduate of the Yale School of Art MFA program and a veteran of the Iraq War.
www.nicholasrock.com

CAMILO SANCHEZ is originally from Bogotá, Colombia, and currently lives in New Jersey. He studied at the School of Visual Arts.
www.macondoconnection.com

CHERMAN QUINO natural born drawer since 1969. i started my graphik karreer in da 70s as a fanatik komik konsumer. in da 90s i get into da amazing underground kulture in lima, peru, inkludes da fanzine *CRASH BOOM ZAP!*
www.cherman.pe

JEISON RODRIGUEZ is an industry art director and graphic designer who continues to stay fresh on the scene with his independent design and printing company WildArtGraphx.com.
www.JeisonRodriguez.com

GORDON SANG I'm an art director/ graphic designer in Chicago. My piece was literally "In Progress" because of procrastination. I was never into politics and rarely designed outside of work— that changed with Obama.
www.nuthinbutagsang.com

HESAM RAHMANIAN is a graduate of Sacramento State University and the School of Visual Arts, Tehran, Iran. He has big dreams—and is moving to bigger cities where he can achieve them faster.
www.studioexperiment.net

RICHARD RODRIGUEZ earned his BFA in printmaking from the Kansas City Art Institute in 2001. He lives in Brooklyn and works as a freelance designer.
www.everyonesinlovewithyou.com

JAMES WILLIAM SCHUYLER III, a native of Philadelphia, documented politically inspired design on obamajawn.com during the 2008 campaign. He is an artist, designer, and craftsman living in Chicago.
www.skilerstudios.com

WEDHA ABDUL RASYID is a graphic artist based in Jakarta, Indonesia.
www.flickr.com/photos/33484920@N04

PAUL ROGERS's illustration clients include the New York Times, Pixar Pictures, and the U.S. Postal Service. His daughter Alexandra was an intern in Obama's presidential campaign office.
www.paulrogersstudio.com

ROBT SEDA-SCHREIBER Not a professional artist, Seda-Schreiber is simply an art teacher with a drawing table at which he sits at times and makes little doodles.
www.sweetestbaboon.blogspot.com

ERIC REWITZER studied at the Cleveland Institute of Art. In 2007 he founded 3 Fish Studios in San Francisco, where he makes paintings and prints based on natural beauty, urban grit, and human diversity.
www.3fishstudios.com

SUSAN ROSSER is a graphic designer from Lighthouse Point, Florida. She attended Muhlenberg College and loves to nap, cook, read, and travel—in that order.
www.rossermarketing.com

CHRIS SEDDON is a professor at Sacramento City College, where he runs the Mac Lab. He instructs students in graphic design, web design, and animation.
www.quirkypixel.com

STUART ROCHFORD was born in Trinidad and Tobago. He is a graphic designer and photographer currently working in Miami.
www.sprochford.com

KAI SALMELA studied graphic design at the University of Minnesota, Duluth, and RISD. He is currently a designer at Pentagram, where he works on print, identity, and environmental design projects.
www.kaisalmela.com

EVA SILVERMAN, a photographer who fell into design after seven years in nonprofits, created Pushcart Design to unite her passions for design and social justice. She supports bringing back the WPA and lives in Oakland.
www.pushcartdesign.com

NICHOLAS SIMSON is an independent designer and supporter of the Obama administration. He is a member of the AIGA and has a BFA in visual communication from Northern Arizona University. www.nicksimson.com

 SHEL STARKMAN is a Hollywood artist/designer. His Hope Obama 08 was selected as a winner out of 1,200 submissions in Shepard Fairey's Manifest Hope competition, and exhibited during the DNC. www.sheldesign.com

 ROLAND TIANGCO Conceived in a Manila summer, born in a Texas winter, and currently living in a room kept cold so he remembers he's not in a womb anymore, Tiangco is a designer working in Brooklyn. www.rolandtiangco.com

 **TOM SLAUGHTER** was born in 1955 in New York City, where he continues to live and work as an artist, designer, and children's book illustrator. His work is included in the public collections of MoMA and the Whitney Museum. www.tomslaughter.com

 **STRAWBERRYLUNA** I am a screen printer and designer living in Pittsburgh, Pennsylvania. I print my work by hand at a community co-op—just me, a squeegee, inks, paper, screens, and a few hours of time. www.strawberryluna.com

 **PHILIP TIDWELL** is an editor and designer for the architecture magazine Pidgin. He studies at Princeton University and has worked as an architectural and graphic designer in Helsinki, Finland; and New York.

 **MARLENA BUCZEK SMITH,** a graduate of the School of Visual Arts, has had her posters exhibited in the United States, Moscow, Milan, and Turkey. www.marlenabuczek.com

 **GONG SZETO** is an independent designer and strategist living in Santa Fe, New Mexico. www.gongszeto.com

 **MARIO TORUNO** I'm a 16-year-old aspiring graphic designer from North Carolina. I love music, reading, television, and Katie Couric. I'm very glad I was able to contribute to our President's election. Yes we did! www.goingdead.net

S. KENNEDY SOBOL is a writer living in Toronto. www.skennedysobol.com

  **MOHAMMAD TAHERI** I like clean, clear, and simple things. I see things in transparencies and put them together to create loud messages. Though I don't live in the States, the future of this world matters to me. www.pictor.us

 **AARON TRASK** is a senior designer at Dragonfly Design Group in Burbank, California. Born and raised in Los Angeles, Aaron does pro bono design work for the Los Angeles County Young Democrats. www.yeswecanposters.org

FELIX SOCKWELL is an illustrator, designer, and regular contributor to the *New York Times* Op Ed, iPhone, and Puzzle sections, among others. Some of his unpublished Obama work was for Penguin Books. www.felixsockwell.com

 **KEVIN TAYLOR** and **BEN GELNETT** Both from Charlotte, North Carolina, Taylor, a designer and illustrator at Radar, and Gelnett, a graphic designer and poster artist at Smackhound, collaborated on this print for Kitschworth. www.kitschworth.com

 **ROBERT TROUTMAN** is a designer who believes in the power of thoughtful, simple design. A RISD graduate, he is the creative director at a studio where he makes things look and feel important. He lives in Fall River, Massachusetts. www.grandfury.com

 **RYAN STAAKE** lives and works in San Francisco's Lower Haight. When not pushing pixels in Silicon Valley, he tries to work on stimulating, culturally relevant projects and is a contributor to the music/culture/design blog Lovelife. www.pompandclout.com

 **WILLIAM THOMAS** was a senior in high school when he designed this poster. He studies computer science Cal Poly Pomona and pursues his passion for website design, specifically PHP and MySQL programming. www.64media.net

 **CHARIS TSEVIS** is an award-winning designer based in Greece. His agency's client list includes companies from all over the globe, including Toyota, IKEA, *Time*, the *Los Angeles Times*, and Saatchi. www.tsevis.com

JEFF WALTERS I am a graphic designer, now at home in Denver (by way of New York City and Ohio), with my cat Bonham and a plate of french fries.

KEITH WEAVER has been a designer and photographer for over 15 years. He lives in Atlanta with his wife and two children.
www.keithweaver.com

AARON WEINSTEIN is a Chicago-based print and web designer. He also maintains www.propagandizer.blogspot.com, an ongoing poster design project.
www.studiostein.com

JOSHUA WENTZ is a Chicago-based designer and musician. His company, Sidedown, is part design agency, part boutique record label, and part publishing imprint.
www.sidedown.com

DONAVON WEST is an independent computer consultant, amateur designer and Microsoft MVP. He lives in Baltimore, Maryland.
www.sidedown.com

ADA WHITNEY, creative director and co-founder of the award-winning New York design studio Beehive. She speaks on title design panels, and has exhibited her paintings and installations extensively.
www.beehive.tv

DAVID YANG was born in Seoul, South Korea, and raised in New York, where he earned a Bachelor of Architecture degree from Cornell University and is pursuing a post-professional Master's of Architecture II at Yale.

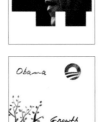

DEBORAH YORK I am a graphic design/arts student at Mission College in Santa Clara, California. I tried to keep the design of my poster simple, refreshing, and to the point.

ACKNOWLEDGMENTS

Thanks to **ADAM MEYER, SPIKE LEE, STEVEN HELLER, VIKKI WARNER, BENEDIKT TASCHEN,** everyone at **TASCHEN** books, and, most importantly, all of the artists who submitted posters. We really accomplished something and I am honored to have been a part of this project and this historic victory.

—AARON PERRY-ZUCKER

Compilation © 2009 Aaron Perry-Zucker and Spike Lee
Aaron Perry-Zucker essay © 2009 Aaron Perry-Zucker
Spike Lee essay © 2009 Spike Lee
Steven Heller essay © 2009 Steven Heller

Any omissions for copy or credit are unintentional and appropriate credit will be given in future editions if such copyright holders contact the publisher.

All images copyright the individual artist. Used with permission. Copyright © Aaron Allen, © Aaron Trask, © Ada Whitney, © Adam C. Morse, © Alex Griendling, © amande.ch, © Ammar Keshodia, © Amos Klausner, © Andrew J. Nilsen, © Andy Hauck, © Barbara Karant/The Grillo Group, Inc., © Bekka Palmer, © Bianca Yvonne Casimes, © Brad Kayal, © Brandon Bailey, © Brandon Kish, © Brendan J. McInerney, © Burkert Design, © Camilo Sanchez, © Caren Litherland, © Charis Tsevis, © CHERMAN revoluchionary grafikz! PERU, © Chigozie Orieh, © Chris Maclean, © Chris Murphy, © Chris Piascik, © Chris Seddon, © Christian Palino, © Christopher Cox/Changethethought, © Christopher Douglas 2008, © Christopher Leal 2009, © Command C Design, © Constantine Giavos, © Corey Favor, © CR Pearce, © Cristiano Andreotti, © Damien Basile, © Dan Almasy 2009, © Darren Newby 2009, © David Yang, © dB, © Deborah York, © Dhari Al-Khaled, © Don Button/RIJATA Design, © Donavon West 2008, © Eddie, © Eric Rewitzer, © Eva Silverman, Pushcart Design, © Felix Sockwell, © fieldsofall.com, © frgdr.com, © Glennys Anglada, Anglada Design, © Gong Szeto, © gongon2, © Gordon Sang, © Graeme Offord, © Hallie Overman, © Hesam Rahmanian, © imflashy.com, © Isaiah King, © Ivette Montes de Oca, Overlap Design, © James Harrison, © James Nesbitt Design, © James William Schuyler III, © Jeff Walters, © Jeison Rodriguez, © Jeremiah Chiu/Plural Design, © Jerry Leibowitz, © Jill Morrison 2008, © Joe Alexander, Lee Dayvault, Corbis/Phil McCarten, © John Derry, © John P. Forrest, Jr., © Joshua Wentz, © Jude Buffum, © Justin Kemerling, © Kai Salmela, © Kaleb Durocher, © Kana Otoma, © Keith Weaver, © Kevin J. Furst, © Kevin J. Gormal, © Kevin Taylor (Radar), © Lagniappe, LLC, © Lee Anne Dollison, LADdesign, © Levi Nicholson, © Lisa Kiss Design, © Mario Toruno 2009, © Maristella Gonzalez, © Marlena Smith 2008, © Matteo Baldarelli, © Michael McMurtrey, © Michelle Farkouh, © Miguel Ayuso, © Mitchell Phillips Design, © Mohammad Taheri 2009, © Mr. Brainwash, © Nicholas DeCarlo, © Nicholas Rock 2008, © nicksimson.com 2008, © Nitin Budhiraja, © Oliva Bernadette Arriola, © Pablo Reyes Pizarro, © Padraig McCobb, © Patrick Gallo/Mike Pintar, © Patrick Macomber, © Paul Rogers, © Paulo Cardoso, © Philip Tidwell, © pio, © Quemadura, © Rafael López, © Renan Molin, © René Garcia, Jr., © Renée Graef, © Richard Perez, © Richard Rodriguez, © Rob Petrullo, © Roberlan Borges 2009, © Robert Finkel, © Robert Troutman, © Robt Seda-Schreiber, © Rodrigo Cortes, © Roland Tiango, © Ryan Byrd, © Ryan Lee Keller, © Ryan Mastalerz, envy creative, © Ryan Staake, © S. Kennedy Sobol, © salvatorelillni.com, © Shell Starkman/Starkmana Design Group, © Sheryl Checkman, © Stephen Phung, © strawberryluna, © Stuart Rochford, © Tom Carmony/Bainbridge Studios LLC 2008, © Tom Slaughter, © Tyreke Hunt, © wedha.ar, © William Thomas, © www.studiostein.com, © Xhengis Aliu, © XK9 Design/Bill Dawson, © Yevgeny Gladun.

IMPRINT

To stay informed about upcoming TASCHEN titles, please request our magazine at www.taschen.com/magazine or write to TASCHEN, Hohenzollernring 53, D-50672 Cologne, Germany, contact@taschen.com, Fax: +49-221-254919. We will be happy to send you a free copy of our magazine which is filled with information about all of our books.

© 2009 TASCHEN GmbH
Hohenzollernring 53
D-50672 Köln
www.taschen.com

Design: Aaron Perry-Zucker, Providence
Art Direction: Josh Baker, Los Angeles
Production: Jennifer Patrick, Los Angeles
Editorial Coordination: Nina Wiener, Los Angeles, and Florian Kobler, Cologne
Design Assistants: Jennifer Hom, Providence, and Marco Zivny, Los Angeles
Project Management: Vikki Warner, Providence, and Mallory Farrugia, Los Angeles
German Translation: Anke Burger, Berlin
French Translation: Alice Pétillot, Paris

Printed in China
ISBN 978-3-8365-1856-7